Photographing Garden Birds

by the same author

*

COLOUR PHOTOMICROGRAPHY
CLOSE-UP COLOUR PHOTOGRAPHY

I. *Great spotted woodpecker.* Cock photographed from the type of hide described on p. 84, using the card shown in Fig. 9 for prefocusing. The bait is a piece of cheese wedged into a crevice of the bark. *Leica* M2, *Visoflex* II, focusing bellows and optical head of the 135-mm. *Elmar* lens at an effective aperture of about f/7. Camera and flash at 4 ft. 3 in. from the bird, with the auxiliary flash head at 4 ft. to light the bird's back. *Kodachrome* I, using a guide number of 30 with a flash set rated at 120 watt-seconds.

Photographing Garden Birds

With a 35-mm Camera

by

C. H. S. TUPHOLME

FABER AND FABER
24 Russell Square
London

*First published in mcmlxii
by Faber and Faber Limited
24 Russell Square London W.C.1
Printed in Great Britain by
Latimer Trend & Co Ltd Plymouth*

Contents

Illustrations

Preface

Bird photography has undoubtedly been an outstanding factor in promoting interest in birds and their welfare, and the frequent publication of articles in magazines and newspapers illustrated not by drawings but by photographs of a very high technical standard and often in colour has done more than anything to make us aware of the bird life around us and its part in the natural beauty of these islands. And to spread knowledge is to foster understanding and sympathy. Bird photography is the most humane of field sports if the photographer bears in mind that his quarry must never be harmed and, if possible, never frightened, especially when nesting. If the photographer intends ultimately to join the ranks of those who stalk wild birds in their haunts, then there is no better place for him to practise than in his own garden or backyard, where the birds will be less disturbed by his activities than the true wild species.

I must emphasize that this is a book about photographing birds in the garden and no attempt is made to instruct the photographer of wild birds in his business. 'My' birds are wild, of course, but many of the situations in which they are photographed are artificially contrived so, strictly speaking, the birds cannot be said to be in their 'natural' state. For instance, a picture of a nuthatch on a peanut-holder could not be said to represent the bird in nature because peanuts are imported and the holder is made by man. However, these birds visit my garden as part of their normal life, I have made a hobby of photographing this phase of their existence and a great deal of fun I've had doing it. In persuading my sitters to pose for me I have added immensely to my store of knowledge of our ordinary English garden birds, and I believe the results of my efforts have been of interest and instruction to my immediate circle of friends and relations. In the course of pursuing this hobby I have never injured a bird or driven one from its nest. Naturally, I have blasphemed at starlings and sparrows and I have even cursed the great spotted woodpecker when he has been disobliging, but none of them seems to have suffered very much as a result.

Some bird photographers concentrate on one species, photographing it at all stages from the egg to full adult plumage, showing it feeding, bathing and in fact in all the normal activities of its life. Such a series can form a most valuable and instructive record. Other photographers collect a series of close-up portraits of individual birds, photographed on such a scale that minute details of the plumage are easily seen. This is my own aim with 35-mm. colour film and is, I suggest, a not unworthy branch of bird photography and very well suited to the man who invites birds to his garden in which the terrain is not so varied as it is for the photographer who stalks the truly wild bird in its natural habitat.

In the following chapters I have tried to pass on some of the many things I have learned in my attempts to bring my 35-mm. camera close enough to the quarry to fill the $1 \times 1\frac{1}{2}$-in. frame with his portrait. This is not so difficult, perhaps, if one has lenses of very long focal lengths, telescopic lenses in fact, but such lenses not only have long focal lengths but very long prices, and the majority of amateurs are, no doubt, like myself, limited by their means in the choice of equipment. My own apparatus consists of an *Exakta* single-lens reflex which is used with either a 135-mm. f/4 *Sonnar* lens for photographing the larger birds, or the optical section of a 105-mm. f/3·5 *Trinol* lens and *Novoflex* bellows for close-ups of small birds. More recently I have acquired a *Leica*, *Visoflex* reflex attachment, focusing bellows and the optical section of a 135-mm. f/4 *Elmar* lens. With this equipment I can obtain an image of any bird, even a wren, large enough to fill the whole frame, if (and it is a big 'if') I can get near enough. But it is not necessary to own all this equipment to take successful bird pictures in colour. The *Leica* is used for ordinary everyday photography, and the *Exakta* for photomacrography and photomicrography. Very good results can be obtained with cheap cameras and the so-called 'portrait' lenses, provided certain elementary rules are observed on the use of such lenses.

As I have already implied, however skilled the photographer may be or however suitable his equipment for the job, he will never succeed unless the welfare of the bird is his first consideration. His aim is to photograph the bird going about its ordinary business, whether sitting on the nest, feeding or bathing, and he cannot do this if he is noisy, clumsy or inconsiderate. This is most important when photographing a sitting or brooding bird because, though this is in many ways the easiest method of securing a photograph, it is also the time when the contents of the nest, whether eggs or young, are most vulnerable to neglect by the parent bird, who may be kept too long away from the nest by a clumsy or selfish photographer. When photographing at feeding or bathing sites, it is of course up to the birds whether they come within camera range or not and the photographer must use his ingenuity to induce them to do so, not just once but again and again. No hardship whatever is done to the birds by this method, which is the one I use most often for my own photographs.

This work is not a bird book, because I am primarily a photographer, and an amateur one at that, and by no means an ornithologist. I have, however, here and there paid attention to the habits and tastes of ordinary garden birds because some such knowledge is fundamental to any success in photographing them. One must, after all, know something about the behaviour of different species before one can decide on the best way to take pictures of them: some always feed on the ground; others will come to a bird table; others again catch their food in mid-air, such as flycatchers, but return time and again to the same perch; and so on. One must perforce arrange oneself and the camera to suit the quarry. The following chapters, therefore, I believe, apply to any garden birds anywhere in the world.

In discussing photographic equipment and accessories I have mentioned the products of only very few makers because it is quite impossible to describe all the many 35-mm. cameras and accessories and the brands of colour reversal and negative material. The examples of equipment chosen for what must be very brief descriptions are taken from both ends of the price scale—the cheap and the costly. I have assumed that no one would buy a camera especially for garden bird photography, but would use the one he already has and would thus be familiar with its characteristics. Unless he has already done a certain amount of close-up work, the photographer must add the appropriate accessories to his equipment, but these need not be expensive.

Finally, anyone who is encouraged to follow my example should join one of the societies whose function it is to encourage interest in birds by disseminating information about them, such as the Royal Society for the Protection of Birds and the British Trust for Ornithology, who publish booklets and pamphlets on birds packed with information and available at very low prices. There are, of course, corresponding societies in overseas countries. Every British ornithologist, too, should make himself familiar with the main provisions of the Protection of Birds Act, 1954.

CHAPTER 1

Introduction

Every keen gardener starts off with or soon acquires an interest in nature, which includes the wildlife frequenting his land: of this wildlife there is no doubt that the birds are the most absorbing, because of their colour and movement, and also because of their often highly individual habits and behaviour. Few people fully realize the entertainment and instruction that ordinary garden birds provide; for example, the blue tits who sometimes seem to indulge in acrobatics for the love of it. In my garden, which is about a third of an acre, though there is enough cover for me to sit and read or write, I find it impossible to concentrate for the bird life going on around me. As soon as I have settled down and the birds have seen me 'anchored', so to speak, and presumably harmless, they carry on with what they were doing when I interrupted them. The robin is always round one's feet, of course, but other birds can be studied at close range: a wren flitting in and out of the low-growing shrubs, chaffinches searching the border and dunnocks, or hedge-sparrows, nearly always in pairs, combing the lawn methodically. The occasional flock of long-tailed tits goes through the trees above, swinging at the ends of the silver birch twigs over my head. The nuthatch, too, is fairly tame and will come close enough to be seen in detail; while the tree-creeper, exploring a tree trunk only a few feet away, ignores me entirely, whether I keep quiet or not. If I keep very still the great spotted woodpecker may fly to his feeding place about 50 ft. away.

MOST BIRDS ARE TIMID

Despite the relative tameness of some species, we must unfortunately accept fear of man as a built-in characteristic of almost all birds. Some, such as the robin and great tit, can be tamed to the point where they will take food from the hand, especially in hard weather, but we don't want to confine our interest to the one or two varieties which are thus easily approached. There is also the added danger that a bird so tamed will exert proprietorial rights and drive others away. We can, however, do much to accustom birds to our presence if, whenever possible, we refrain from unnecessary sudden movement when they can see us. Perhaps thousands of previous generations have conditioned birds to associate sudden movement with the moment of supreme danger when being stalked: even turning the head quickly in their direction is often enough to frighten birds away. On the other hand, they do not seem to mind sudden noise if it is not too near. I have shovelled coke into a hod within 20 ft. of a great spotted woodpecker feeding without driving him away; but this was because I have been hidden by a screen of wooden panels which enclose the coke bin. On the other hand, the noise of the shutter of a partly-hidden camera a few feet away has disturbed him though, if the bait is tempting enough, he generally returns before very long. On other occasions he scuttles quickly round the tree trunk and returns when he thinks all is clear. When this happens I have to let him feed in peace because I can't get at the camera to wind the shutter without driving him off.

The lesson of all this is that, though one must necessarily move about the garden and for most of the time in full view of the birds, one should whenever possible do so quietly. One can pass quite near a timid bird provided one continues uninterruptedly on one's way, but to stop except behind cover at once rouses the bird's suspicions; and to stop and turn the head in his direction is usually fatal. To sum up my own experience, I would say that the way to keep the birds one has attracted is to move about the garden as silently as possible; at least to appear to be absorbed in one's own ploys; and, to all intents and purposes, to ignore them. If this can be done, it is surprising how many birds will accept one as being a part of the garden furniture.

Introduction

SHOULD BIRDS BE ENCOURAGED?

Many people hesitate to encourage birds because, they say, they do enough damage in the garden already without any inducement to come more often and in greater numbers. I, for one, don't believe this to be true. Of course, tits will rob green-pea pods, jays will take broad beans and both blackbirds and thrushes will steal soft fruit and will scatter soil on the paths in their search for worms along the border, especially in dry weather. But they would do this anyway, and I believe they are less likely to rob the garden if plenty of other natural or artificial food is provided. I protect my green peas with glitterbangs and I net the broad beans and I don't lose any at all. Some birds will come to a garden in any case and, if nothing is provided for them, they will take what's there. One would hardly say that the French and other continental fruit-growers are less careful of their crops than those in Britain, and in Europe one often sees the insectivorous birds encouraged by the provision of nesting boxes, bird tables and the like. Of course, one has to sweep the path after a blackbird or thrush has been hunting, but the mess they make is more than compensated for by their song which, in the case of the thrush, continues daily during the winter when all else is silent and dreary. As for the other common garden birds, robins, dunnocks and chaffinches, they do absolutely no harm at any season of the year.

There has, on the other hand, been a great deal published, much of this from official sources, on the good wrought by birds. One has only to watch the feeding of nestlings to realize to what extent birds help to rid the garden of those almost unseen (by us) pests which wreak so much damage. One of my neighbours complains that the great spotted woodpecker I encourage pecks large holes in his rose pergola posts. So it does in mine, and if I'd paid more attention to these warnings a few years ago and renewed some of the posts this woodpecker had marked for me, I would not have been confronted one morning with half the pergola blown flat by a gale in the night.

Thanks largely to the B.B.C., the British Trust for Ornithology and the Royal Society for the Protection of Birds, the increase in the number of bird-lovers, especially among the young, has been phenomenal. And with greater interest in, and knowledge of, birds has come a greater affection for them, an understanding of their way of life with a desire to protect them and to supply them so far as possible with what they need. This very desirable improvement in our attitude to birds is by no means so widespread as it should be but, aided by education and the law, it is growing rapidly.

A GOOD BIRD BOOK IS ESSENTIAL

Every garden bird photographer should have a good bird book with accurate colour reproductions so that he can at once identify any new arrival and add to the knowledge he will have gained from his own observations of the species frequenting his garden. There are many such books and it is worth while examining them well before purchase because they do differ in the precise colouring of a species, and a decision is best made after examining the illustrations of the commoner birds to see whether their colours match the photographer's observation. If the colour renderings of the cock chaffinch, greenfinch and the robin in winter plumage agree with what the observer himself has seen, it may be assumed that the colour printing throughout is good.

Though all birds of one species, with very few exceptions, have almost identical colouring, they do vary quite widely in behaviour and it will be found that regular visitors to the feeding sites are easily identified. For example, a one-legged jay ('Long John Silver') has been a constant visitor to our garden for several years and the way he has mastered his handicap is much to be admired. One great tit has a drooping wing, though his flight is quite normal. A cock blackbird has a much rounder head than the others of his tribe. And many birds—far too many—seem to suffer from some deformity of leg or foot. Most observers interested in the study of garden birds and their habits will find it easy to become sentimental about them: to attribute to them human emotions, behaviour and ways of thinking.

BIRDS AND COLOUR PHOTOGRAPHY

If one is a photographer as well as a bird-lover one will be

Introduction

prompted by the urge to capture these beautiful creatures on film for one's collection and also, perhaps, to provide friends with proof of the rare or unusual birds one has succeeded in attracting to the garden. The growing understanding of birds has been accompanied by an increase in colour photography, especially in the 35-mm. size. Undoubtedly colour photography is at its best when nature is the subject, and birds are no less a 'natural' for colour photography than flowers. Only colour photography can capture the subtle difference in hue in a single feather in the commonest of garden birds. That spiv of the bird world, the starling, is a case in point. When feeding on the lawn, he appears a sort of dull brown. Yet, when photographed close-up in colour it is seen that he is in fact predominantly a glossy black with iridescent spots of blue, purple and green. To capture his quarry the garden bird photographer must either take his camera to the birds in their haunts or attract them to sites for feeding, bathing or nesting. Of these two methods the second is easier, far more reliable and productive of much more satisfactory results. In either case he must arrange to have himself and his camera or the camera alone at the right place at the right time. This may sound a pretty tall order but it is in fact much easier to do than it sounds, as I hope to show in succeeding chapters.

CHAPTER 2

Attracting Birds

To be able to photograph birds one must first induce them to frequent the garden, and the number of bird species that can be attracted either to nest or to feed, or both, does not depend primarily upon the size of the garden, but much more upon the kind of place they are invited to. There are records of very small town and suburban gardens in which as many as twenty different kinds of birds are regularly seen, and what I have to say on the subject of attracting wild birds applies mainly to those who like myself have gardens of between a quarter and a half acre, though the owner of a plot smaller than this can reasonably expect to attract all the species who now use my garden for feeding, bathing or nesting, if he provides them with their chief needs. Even the owner of a backyard will succeed in attracting some birds, particularly the tits, if he fixes nest boxes and feeding devices well away from the ground and other jumping-off places for cats. If the small garden or backyard happens to be near a park or allotments he can confidently expect the birds to nest because the open spaces will give them a hunting ground for the caterpillars and grubs which are part of the diet of nestlings.

GARDENS SHOULDN'T BE TOO TIDY

Too tidy a garden will not encourage birds to take up their quarters, though they may come to feed. It is generally possible, however, in most gardens in the suburbs and even in some towns, to have a corner which can be left 'natural'. This does not mean an untidy tangle to constitute an eyesore, but if a few suitable shrubs can be planted some birds will nest. Such shrubs should

22

not be treated as so-called 'specimen' trees and given solitary positions dotted about the lawn, but should be clustered in one small area. Quick-growing varieties are privet and cupressus lawsoniana, which can be clipped to provide close cover. A box bush, though a slower grower, will provide nesting sites for small birds. If the garden has been carved out of the wild, so to speak, it may contain a gorse bush or two and perhaps a few brambles. If these can be preserved, say in a quiet corner of the garden, the long-tailed tit may be persuaded to stay.

When I first came to this district the countryside was much more open than it is now. There were fewer houses and the common land of which this part of Surrey was so largely composed provided cover for a very wide variety of bird life. This garden, a little over a quarter-acre, was once part of common land and the previous owner, fortunately, had preserved a group of silver birches which form a kind of small copse. During my first year here thirty-seven different species used the garden for feeding or nesting and the nightingale and nightjar were regularly heard. However, we are now virtually an outer suburb of London, all land in the immediate vicinity of the house being built upon, while across the canal at the end of the garden and within 100 yards is a large L.C.C. housing estate. Naturally, the nightingale and some others have deserted us, but we still have the occasional flock of goldfinches feeding on the lawn, and groups of long-tailed tits working their way through the treetops.

Our birches have been underplanted with several quick-growing rhododendron ponticum, and around the bases of these and of the trees the grass is allowed to grow long so that an occasional willow warbler's or robin's nest is found. By planting one corner of dwarf trees and shrubs to provide cover, and by leaving one small part of the garden in a kind of orderly disorder, we have managed to continue to offer hospitality to many birds, while others, such as the great spotted woodpecker and the nuthatch, though they nest elsewhere, come regularly to us to feed.

TREES AND SHRUBS FOR NESTS

A close-growing hedge provides suitable cover for the shy

dunnock or hedge-sparrow and I have found their nests in a row of berberis stenophylla and in two large box bushes which have been allowed to grow to about 5 ft. Chaffinches seem to prefer a rather more open site and a favourite spot is somewhere along the top of a row of the rose *Albertine,* which has been trained to form a 4-ft. hedge dividing off a very small kitchen garden. Blackbirds, thrushes and chaffinches build in a row of cupressus lawsoniana forming a boundary; and wrens have built in a climbing rose growing thickly against a post. Robins, of course, will build in the most absurd places. My nest boxes are regularly occupied by blue or great tits; and for three years running a pair of spotted fly-catchers used an open-sided box against the wall of the house amongst the branches of a climbing rose. The first two years they nested inside the box in the orthodox way: in the third season they built on top of the box. Unfortunately, we have a large sparrow population and after the third year the flycatchers gave up in disgust and moved to a more select neighbourhood.

More often than not, when buying a house and garden, one inherits a number of trees and shrubs and if the previous owner happened to be interested in encouraging birds one will indeed be fortunate because the place will already offer natural shelter or food and sometimes both. In most cases, however, if a really serious attempt is to be made to bring birds to the garden, some adjustments will be necessary and the extent of these will naturally be governed by the space available. Most English gardens are relatively small, but this is no disadvantage and room can be found for shrubs and trees which beautify the garden and also attract birds. Some of these if already present can be improved by pruning to provide a closer growth and, if new specimens are planted, they should as a rule be of quick-growing varieties.

FOOD AND COVER

Of the two attractions to birds, I believe a tree which gives cover is preferred to one that offers food only. Both the quick-growing cypresses for hedging, macrocarpa and lawsoniana, pro-vide no food but do offer good cover and building sites. Of the two, lawsoniana is the more dependable. Macrocarpa will flourish

II. *Chaffinch.* Photograph of a cock at the bait described on pp. 34 and 106. Taken through window glass with *Exakta*, *Novoflex* bellows and optical section of 105-mm. *Trinol* lens. *Kodachrome* I at a guide number of 28 with a 120-watt-sec electronic flash. No auxiliary head used.

for a few years and may then suddenly die out. Moreover, it is not really suitable for a district where severe frosts are experienced. Holly and yew are excellent windbreaks and cover trees and the berries are welcome food. If one has a beech tree in the garden, it will be found that the mast is liked by a number of birds and so it is, unfortunately, by the squirrel. Woodpecker species often make their nesting holes in beech forests.

The ordinary crab, besides being ornamental, will, if properly pruned, form a dense tree, giving cover to birds of all sizes. The fruit, too, is eaten. I have a crab on the lawn not far from the window where I do my 'internal' photography. It is an exceedingly popular jumping-off ground for birds approaching the photographic bait just outside the window, and its rough bark has provided the great spotted woodpecker with a number of cracks and holes where he lodges nuts and other food when eating. The almond tree provides almost no cover, but the nuts are popular with these woodpeckers. An almond tree is well worth having as an ornament, being one of the earliest to flower, but I don't think it is worth while planting solely for the benefit of the woodpeckers. They will in any case remove the nuts and wedge them into some kind of crevice for cracking and, that being the case, one might just as well buy the almonds, do the wedging for them and use the nuts as a bait for photography. I have done this and I have also bought Brazil nuts for the same purpose. These nuts are tough to crack and keep the great spotted woodpecker in one place long enough to be photographed. Once he has opened the nut, he is very rarely able to remove the kernel whole and fly away with it so, when he has had his fill, a nuthatch may come on the scene and after him one of the ubiquitous tit family. Hazel nuts are popular with woodpeckers and nuthatches, but the same arguments apply here as in the case of the almond tree. The nut must always be removed by the bird and eaten elsewhere.

One must, incidentally, be prepared for what seems to be quite illogical behaviour on the part of many birds. I have mentioned that my crab tree has a number of natural holes and crevices in the bark where the great spotted woodpecker will wedge a nut. But quite often he will ignore a perfectly well-shaped hole of the right size and proceed to enlarge a smaller one. He first of all searches the tree with the nut in his beak to find a hole which he considers suitable for enlarging. He then gets to work and, since he cannot hold the nut and peck at the hole at the same time, he wedges the nut with his chest against the tree. Had he left the nut, which I had already firmly fixed, or so I thought, in a suitable hole on which I had the camera focused, he could have got his meal and I my picture much sooner, but things don't always work this way. The nuthatch, on the other hand, is much more obliging and will usually eat the nut where he finds it.

BERRIED SHRUBS

Many of the berrying shrubs will attract birds. Almost all of the berberis family provide food and *B. stenophylla*, the very prickly one, not only makes a lovely hedge ablaze in the early spring with deep golden flowers, but offers nesting sites. The cotoneasters, being rather loose-growing, do not offer shelter but they do provide food. Cotoneaster horizontalis, which grows flat against a wall, provides food and it also has another advantage. In the early spring the minute flowers attract queen wasps and, if these are watched for and destroyed, the wasp population of the garden later in the year will be much reduced.

If the 'wild' corner of the garden is a practicable proposition, the tangle will offer food, nesting sites and shelter to many small birds. Gorse, whether of the larger variety (*Ulex europaeus*) or dwarf (*U. nanus*), is a candidate for this corner and several varieties of small birds may nest in it. The long-tailed tit seems to prefer the kind of prickly cover given by this shrub, or a willow warbler's nest may be found in the rough grass round the base of the stem. The common hawthorn seems to be a more popular larder with birds than the more ornamental cultivated varieties. This may be because the two species of the wild variety, being more often seen, are better known to birds, or because the hybridists in improving the blossom have spoilt the fruit. Hawthorn will make a very good hedge, sometimes acceptable in the most precise of gardens, and if so will provide cover as well as food. Some birds are very fond of elderberries, so, though the elder can hardly be called a garden shrub, if already established it should, if possible, be left. One grows on the canal bank at the end of my garden and it has been shaped to a not unattractive small tree, thriving in a situation where nothing else can survive except alders and some bamboo. The berries are highly prized by some birds. The ordinary blackberry is popular as a source of food. If the bush can be 'compacted', so to speak, by training and pruning so that it will form a close and very prickly mass, some small birds may nest in it.

PLANT SEEDS

The seeds of many annual and perennial plants are attractive to seedeaters and among them are the annual and perennial asters and marigolds, especially of the dwarf French variety. Sunflowers are great favourites especially with the tits, who often take the seed before it is fully ripe, unless the head is removed as soon as the seed starts to change colour and hung up out of harm's way: for this an open shed or one of which the door is left open for an appreciable part of the day is no use at all. The tits will soon find it and the seed will rapidly disappear. A greenhouse is ideal.

CLIMBING PLANTS

Many thickly-growing climbers offer shelter and nesting sites. If ivy and ampelopsis are grown against a high wall the birds may build near the top, thus presenting difficulties for the photographer, but one of these climbers on the side of a brick garage, toolshed or other low building is ideal for nest photography. Wild honeysuckle offers nesting sites, but unfortunately some cultivated varieties also harbour greenfly and blackfly who soon make the leaves and flowers unsightly. Tits feed on the fly, of course, but do not seem to make really serious inroads on their numbers. The ordinary wild honeysuckle suffers less in this respect and, where it can be kept under control, is worth having. Both pyracantha and mountain ash provide berried food and in the former, which grows thickly against a wall, a nest will often be found.

When thinking of natural cover we must not overlook those places which can be contrived by any thoughtful property owner.

Attracting Birds

Every garden should have some kind of untidy corner in addition to the wild piece referred to, where there is perhaps a small lean-to or lengths of timber stacked against a tree. If the toolshed is boarded, an occasional gap can be left, or one end of a board wedged out in such a way that a small bird can find its way in and build between the inner and outer linings of the structure. In all such cases, unfortunately, one has to contend with rats, especially near water, but these can be dealt with by one of the *Warfarin* poisons. When birch brooms become too worn to be of further use, they can be wired in an upright position in some secluded part of the garden. Blackbirds seem very fond of building on top of the worn-down twigs.

LAWNS

An important attraction to birds is, fortunately, of equal attraction to the garden-owners, and that is a regularly mown lawn. Even a few minutes' observation will show that more birds spend more time on short grass hunting for food than they do on any other part of the garden. I have a stretch of rough grass, sickled only twice a year, under the silver birches, and it is noticeable that almost no birds are to be seen on the ground here except when searching for nesting sites or materials, though the mown grass attracts robins, blackbirds, thrushes, dunnocks, members of the finch family and the green woodpecker.

So far as lawns are concerned no one who wishes to encourage birds should use a chemical wormkiller on his grass because any worms so destroyed and afterwards eaten by a bird will act as a poison and may lead to the bird's death. In this connection an article by P. J. Conder in *Bird Notes*, No. 3, Summer 1960, published by the R.S.P.B., describes the disaster to robins in the U.S.A. as a result of eating poisoned worms. It appears that elms that had been sprayed against Dutch elm disease duly shed their leaves, which were eaten by earthworms during the winter. These worms had accumulated and concentrated the D.D.T. in their bodies and were eaten by robins in the spring with the result that some of the heavily-sprayed suburbs of Detroit, Milwaukee and Chicago were subsequently reported to have practically no robins.

Attracting Birds

These birds were not the only ones poisoned by the D.D.T. spray: many other ground-feeders were killed and so were birds which feed on insects they find in tree bark, including woodpeckers, tits, nuthatches and tree-creepers. If leaves from unsprayed trees fall on the grass, however, there is no danger of poisoning. Even if they are not immediately swept up, a number will be removed by worms, and any increase in the worm population is an encouragement to the birds.

WATER FOR DRINKING AND BATHING

A constant supply of water is every bit as necessary to birds as food, not only for drinking but for bathing. As in feeding, some birds seem to prefer drinking or bathing at ground level, such as in a pond; and others only feel happy when drinking or bathing above ground, as on a pedestal-type birdbath or in a dish. If birds used the water only for drinking, a small dish on the bird table would be the answer, but some of them may insist on bathing in it, thus splashing and soaking any food present.

An excellent way to provide birds with water is to have a garden pond which not only supplies them with drinking and bathing water, but also provides a focal point of interest in any garden. To do this, the pond should have one or two water-lilies, which require a depth of water of between 2 ft. and 3 ft. In my case, this depth is supplied by depressions in the floor of the pond to form a kind of basin, the rest of the pond being shallower. This form of construction has the advantage that soil and leaves, which inevitably find their way into the water, tend to gravitate to these basins so that the water-lily roots are supplied with cover and nourishment. My pond (Fig. 1) is of irregular shape about 12 ft. long and 6 ft. wide and accommodates two water-lilies— *escarboucle*, a rich red, and *odorata*, almost pure white. Some fish are kept to add interest and to feed on the larvae of flying—and stinging—insects. A place for the birds to drink and bath has been provided by building a kind of underwater lean-to at one end, the end nearest my toolshed, which also serves as a permanent hide to photograph birds bathing. Two or three flat stones, supported by bricks, lie an inch or so below the water surface when the pond is

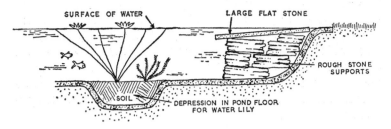

FIG. 1. Section of one end of the pond showing the flat stone used by birds for bathing. How this bathing place is used for photography is seen in Fig. 5a.

full and there is a shallow and a deep end to oblige birds of all sizes. This structure not only provides the birds with somewhere to bath, but also gives the fish shelter in the winter when there are no water-lily leaves under which they can hide. Some oxygenating plants should be installed and one or two water snails to help clear the water.

The pond should be in a semi-open position. That is to say, it should not be under trees because it will collect the falling leaves in the autumn and the water will become fouled. On the other hand, it should not stand right out in the open because anyone who watches his garden birds will soon discover that birds very rarely fly direct to food or water. They prefer to alight on a perch near by to reconnoitre the surroundings. There should not be low-growing dense shrubs too near the pond because these will give cover to an enemy. My pond has a wide lawn on one side of it, a narrow path on the other and beyond that a few evergreen shrubs, such as laurustinus and pernettya, to which the birds can fly and hide if they are disturbed.

A pond of any size will supply most birds' needs but, if there is no room for one, a birdbath will do. This should be placed in much the same kind of situation as the pond and should be cleaned regularly with a stiff brush and kept topped up. Ready-made birdbaths may be bought, either for standing on the ground or mounted on a pedestal, or one can be made from a discarded kitchen sink, large baking-tin, oven tin or some similar receptacle. These home-made birdbaths are, for the sake of appearance, best sunk into the ground and, if they are new and bright, they should be painted inside and out with some corrosion-resisting paint, which will also help to give them a more natural appearance than bright new tin. It is most essential that birdbaths should not be too deep and it is a good plan to arrange them so that the water is, say, 1 in. deep at one end and about 2 in. deep at the other. This can be done by placing flat stones in the bath to regulate the level. Birdbaths should always be sited well away from bushes and other cover for enemies, though a small tree near by will be appreciated as a jumping-off ground and as a perch where birds can preen themselves after bathing.

Artificial Foods

There is some difference of opinion on the artificial feeding of garden birds. At one extreme is the view of some ornithologists that birds should be fed in the winter only and that feeding during the other seasons may even be harmful. At the other is the opinion that one cannot give birds too much: in fact, they need as much as they can get because they are always hungry, or so it appears. I think the truth lies between these extremes. I have never confined feeding to the winter because during the rest of the year the birds would lack this powerful inducement to live in my garden. But I do think that birds are best fed by not being given too much of one kind of food at certain times of the year. For example, I do not provide so much bread when young are being fed in the nest. The same applies to live maggots or, as fishermen call them, gentles. They are the larvae of bluebottles and, while they are of benefit to adult birds, they are known to be harmful to nestlings. I have never been able to bring myself to breed gentles, but it is possible to do so provided one realizes that one is taking the risk of increasing the bluebottle population. If they are required they can be bought from dealers who breed them specially for cage-bird fanciers and anglers. A form of live food which, however, can be bred is the mealworm, a beetle larva. This also can be bought in pet shops.

LIVE FOODS

If one is a gardener, one will come across all kinds of live foods which birds appreciate, such as woodlice, caterpillars, ants' eggs, earthworms and snails. These can be put in suitable containers and placed on the bird table or some other spot easily accessible to birds. Snails, for instance, can be dropped into a tin on the ground for the benefit of thrushes and, if a stone to serve as an anvil is put near by, it might be possible to get close-ups of thrushes in action. So far as earthworms are concerned, I have never been able to bring myself to thread one on a fish-hook, much less cut it up for the birds. These worms do a great deal of good in the garden and I feel that if the birds want them they must be about the lawn or other parts of the garden early and catch them for themselves.

Other types of natural food abound in the garden at certain seasons. Caterpillars and ants are examples. Apparently the smaller birds leave the hairy types of caterpillar alone, which is understandable. And no bird, in my garden at any rate, will touch the caterpillar of the cabbage white butterfly, probably because of its reputedly bitter flavour, so this pest must be dealt with oneself. The green woodpecker is a great anteater, and flycatchers hunt them in the flying stage, as do some other small birds with varying degrees of success. I have sometimes set up my hide hopefully near an ants' nest on the chance that a green woodpecker will come along, but I've had no luck, though he makes frequent visits to the lawn which is laid on sand and therefore infested with ants.

HOUSEHOLD SCRAPS AND SPECIAL FOODS

These and many other natural foods must at certain times of the year be supplemented by household scraps, left-overs and so on. Bread, on the whole, is not good for birds and, if other food is available it will be noticed that the bread, especially if white, will be left until last. Breadcrumbs or crusts can be mixed with other scraps, but not, if it can be avoided, when nestlings are being fed. Dry crusts should not be soaked but crushed to tiny pieces

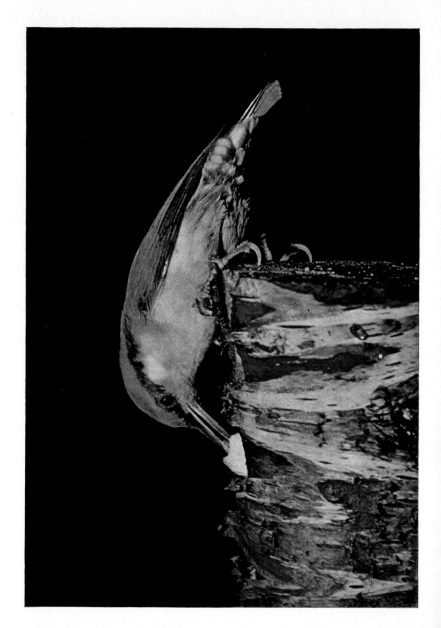

III. *Nuthatch.* Characteristic attitude on the bait described on p. 109. He is about to extract a peanut from its shell. Photographed through window glass with *Exakta, Novoflex* bellows and optical head of 105-mm. *Trinol* lens. Camera and flash 2 ft. 9 in. from the bird, with the auxiliary flash at 4 ft. to light the bird's back. *Kodachrome* I, guide number 30 with 120-watt-sec flash.

before being offered. Brown or wholemeal bread is more nourishing than white and stale cake crumbs are a better food than both during the nesting season because it has the higher protein content that the young birds need before they are fledged.

There is some difference of opinion on the value of coco-nuts. Some say this food is harmful to very young birds but there is no doubt that it is a great favourite with all the tits, nuthatches and woodpeckers. The nut should be sawn in half and hung up so that water does not lodge in it. Apart from the seeds naturally available in the garden, one can buy packets of made-up mixtures on sale for pets or wild birds. These generally contain an assortment from which each bird can make his choice. Or one can buy hemp seed and linseed by weight. I find nearly all birds like hemp, but on the single occasion when I spread linseed on the ground the birds ignored it. I feed hemp by putting some in an empty coco-nut shell for the table-feeders and spread some on the lawn for the dunnocks and others who prefer to feed on the ground. Hemp, of course, is one of the heating foods and should not be fed to the birds during summer.

My most popular bait is cheese, which all birds take avidly all the year round. The larger pieces are put into the round tin with a wire bottom described in the next paragraph for the tits, nuthatches, great spotted woodpeckers and the occasional starling who has mastered the trick of hanging upside down. The smaller pieces are put on a bird table covered with 1½-in. mesh wire for the smaller birds; and the rest is scattered on the lawn for all-comers. Of any food put out, cheese is always the first to go. I might add, incidentally, that the birds' preference is for Cheddar. Cheshire is unpopular and so is Danish Blue!

At first I put pieces of cheese and other titbits in a circular basket made of ½-in. mesh wire with a hinged lid of the same material, but the starlings could secure a foothold on the wire and took all the cheese. To circumvent these birds, I cut the bottom out of a large round tin and replaced it with ½-in. mesh wire through which the birds can reach the cheese. This tin, painted green, is tied against the trunk of a tree, the lid being used to protect the contents from wet. The great spotted woodpecker visits this regularly, the tree trunk underneath the tin providing him with a foothold while he feeds. The smooth sides of the tin prevent any bird from gripping it while feeding, but the tits and nuthatches hang upside down on the wire at the bottom and one or two starlings have also discovered how to do this, but they feel insecure and never stay very long.

A more sightly feeder, designed for the great spotted woodpecker, was specially made for me by Birdcraft Products, of Woodford Green, Essex. It consists of a bored-out smooth-barked log with a cover made in two parts—a flat roof to which is screwed a circular wooden plate which fits inside the bore, being held in position by a long brass pin passing right through the assembly so that the feeder can be suspended by the hook at the top. When replenishing the food supply, the brass pin is withdrawn and the feeder section lowered. Square ¼-in. mesh wire is fixed inside the bore about ½ in. from the bottom so that it is out of sight. Suspended against the trunk of a weeping cherry this feeder, which is shown in section in Fig. 2, is quite inconspicuous.

One of my most successful baits for small birds is a short piece of alder, hollowed out at the top to make a cup about 2 in. wide and 1 in. deep. The alder is fixed to the top of a bamboo cane stuck into the ground a few inches from the dining-room window and the 'cup', filled with cheese, regularly attracts four species of tits, greenfinches, chaffinches and nuthatches to a spot near enough for a real close-up to be taken through the window. This cheese has also been visited by a willow warbler and, in hard weather, wrens and water wagtails.

BIRD TABLES

There is almost as great a variety of bird tables as there is of nest boxes and the type or types chosen must be governed by the kind of bird one hopes to entice. One can buy tables of the most elaborate design and many of them are most attractive and effective. However, I've always found the simple kind of tray as good as any. I have only one and this is a 2 × 1-ft. platform provided with a plain sloping roof so that wet can run off. I do no photography at all of birds on the table, but confine my picture-taking to the special devices set up at various points near the house

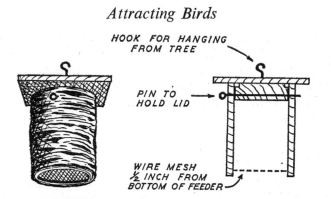

HOOK FOR HANGING
FROM TREE

PIN TO
HOLD LID

WIRE MESH
½ INCH FROM
BOTTOM OF FEEDER

FIG. 2. Rustic feeding device for great spotted woodpeckers specially made for the author by Birdcraft Products from a length of smooth-barked tree bored out to form a cylinder.

because they have been specially designed to meet the requirements of close-up photography.

Whatever type of bird table is chosen, its situation is very important. It should, of course, be near the house or near the other feeding devices set up for photographic purposes. It should be placed near cover but not near the ground with dense bushes near by, and it should if possible be supported in such a way that there is no easy foothold for enemies. My own bird table seems to suit its customers very well. It is fixed at the top of the very smooth stem of a standard weeping cherry, so that the birds have a clear view of the surrounding lawn, while the branches immediately over the table give the birds instant cover if they are disturbed, and a convenient approach to the food as well.

Bird tables should be covered with some kind of roof to keep the food dry and a shallow rim to prevent it from being scattered. But, unless one wishes to photograph a number of birds feeding, such a table is not ideal for photography. Unless it is quite small in area depth of field problems will arise and the roof, of course, decreases the amount of 'photographic' light falling on the birds. Again, it will generally be found that the larger birds will drive the small ones away and, if starlings infest the garden, they will get all the food. The best use for such a table is to entice the birds near the house and, to keep the starlings off, I have wired mine overall with 1½-in. mesh wire, including a rough door. This keeps

35

out blackbirds and thrushes, unfortunately, so they are fed by scattering food on the lawn near my feet, my presence at the time being enough to keep the starlings at a distance. As soon as I return indoors, however, these birds descend from the tree tops, television aerials and other observation posts and all food soon disappears.

PEANUT HOLDERS

One commonly sees peanuts strung like a bead necklace hanging from the bird table or other support. Nuts offered in this way do attract the tits and occasionally other birds, but one has only to see the string spinning round and round as a bird works on a nut to realize that this kind of bait is far from ideal for photography. Not only does the line of nuts spin and sway, but one can never tell at which point the bird will alight. A better form of peanut bait, I think, is the one I use myself. I have several short lengths of split log into which I have drilled holes $\frac{5}{8}$ in. and $\frac{3}{4}$ in. diameter and about $1\frac{1}{2}$ in. deep, into which the peanuts are wedged tightly so that they are not easily pulled out whole, forcing the bird to open the shell on the spot. When no photography is contemplated I keep most of the holes filled with nuts to maintain the birds' interest. This device attracts not only the tits, but also the great spotted woodpecker and nuthatch. Between these holes are others about $\frac{1}{4}$ in. diameter into which I push shelled nuts. When setting up for photography, I prefocus the camera on one area of the log containing, say, three or four holes occupied by nuts, the others being empty. I can in this way be certain that a bird feeding on this bait will be within the camera's field of view.

The peanut shell, while tough enough to keep a great tit or nuthatch hammering for some minutes, presents no problem to the woodpecker. Two or three blows from his powerful beak are enough to expose the nut, which he generally carries off to some other part of the tree where he wedges it in the rough bark. But some nuts keep him busy for longer and thus make him easier to photograph. There are deep fissures in the bark of my crab tree and into one of these I push very firmly a Brazil nut, but I do help him by first of all cracking the nut carefully. The nut is too firmly

36

wedged for him to carry away entire and, since he can only remove the shell a very small piece at a time, I have him in one position for long enough to photograph, the camera, of course, being pre-focused on the spot. The nuthatch can be photographed in the same way, though in his case I use a hazel nut or a peanut.

SPECIAL FEEDING DEVICES

One can buy special devices for feeding birds most of which are quite efficient and probably better to look at than many home-made articles. Special designs are available for peanuts, fats and seeds. However, so far as peanuts are concerned, I prefer my own arrangement because it does show the nut-eater in natural action: he must crack the shell to get at the nut itself, and it seems to me that, if he can do this and fly away with a whole nut, it is no more than his due reward. I use empty coco-nut shells for both seed and fat. The coco-nut to hold the seed has a 3-in. nail through the base and this fits into the hollow part of an ordinary garden bamboo cane stuck into the ground so that the coco-nut is firmly held. I have used this device for photographing greenfinches and chaffinches. The goldfinch and the dunnock are rather more difficult. They are both ground feeders, so photography is difficult, and the goldfinch seems not to be able to manage an entire hemp seed, so those I throw on the lawn I crack first with an ordinary pastry roller. When using a half coco-nut for fat, I collect the scraps together and melt them down, pouring them into the nut. When the fat has set I hang the coco-nut upside down by a piece of wire, keeping the contents dry.

NEST BOXES

If they can be afforded, nesting boxes specially designed for different bird species can be bought (Fig. 3). If not, they can be made quite easily, provided certain basic rules are observed. In the first place, hardwood is better than soft as it lasts longer. Secondly, wood of adequate thickness should be used because of the insulation it affords against both heat and cold. If the wood is too thin, it may split and the box will in any case too easily become

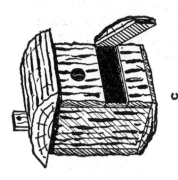

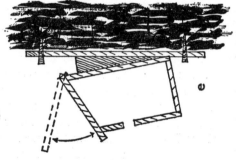

Fig. 3. Types of nest boxes which have proved successful in the author's garden. Box *A* for tits has a removable lower section. Box *B* is for such birds as robins, flycatchers and other birds building in open-fronted sites. Box *C* is for tits and has a hinged section which swings out. These three boxes are made by Birdcraft Products. Box *D*, which is shown in section at *E*, is made for the Royal Society for the Protection of Birds by Scottish war-blinded ex-Servicemen.

hot in summer and, if it is used for shelter in the winter, as it may well be, it will not keep out the cold. Wood of 1 in. thickness is best but it should not be thinner than ¾ in. Third, no vertical joints between the four sides of the box should be uncovered at the top edge because of damp lodging in the crevice and working down into the box. This point is taken care of if the roof is flat and large enough to cover the whole top of the box with a slight overhang, say of ½ in. or so, on both sides and 2 in. in front to give some shade to the entrance hole. It is a good plan to use screws in the construction and to grease them before they are driven home, so that removal is made easier. It is also wise to coat the joints with a plastic sealing compound before screwing up to make absolutely certain of watertightness.

These are the prime considerations in the construction of the box itself, but there are other important points. The box should not be fixed directly to the support, but via a vertical batten, because if the back of the box itself is against a tree or post, water running down the support may seep into the box. The batten should be a vertical one because the water will run off more easily than if a horizontal batten is used. It is also a good plan to fix the box in an inclined position so that its top is farther away from the tree than the bottom. This will ensure that water runs off the top and that the entrance hole, which will face slightly downward, will be more shaded.

Many boxes are made to open, either to satisfy curiosity or for scientific ornithological reasons. For garden purposes, however, I think it much better to leave the birds entirely at peace while they are nesting. A door is a constant temptation to have a peep and any opening surface means that there will be at least one, perhaps four, untight joints, which may let in damp and draught. For my own part, I screw all the surfaces of my boxes up tight with brass screws dipped in graphite and, when the autumn comes, I unscrew the front to clean out and disinfect the box. However, if one must have a door, the front of the box is perhaps the best side to hinge because it will be found that the birds are more likely to make the bed of the nest against the back and away from the entrance. If the front is opened, then, it is unlikely that either eggs or young will fall out. Some boxes are offered with a hinging roof.

This is very convenient for an observer and nothing can fall out if the top is opened, but I feel that unless the hinged joint is well designed, there is the possibility of moisture seeping through. There are some such boxes, however, which are perfectly sound and watertight.

ENTRANCE HOLES

There are two other important points: the first is the location of the entrance hole and its size. The best place for the hole is on the front of the box, away from the tree or other support and therefore less convenient for the would-be predator. The hole, too, should be near the top, say about 2 in. from the roof so as to give the maximum effective depth to the box. So far as the diameter of the hole is concerned, most holes are made too large, so that a box intended for small birds such as tits and nuthatches is appropriated by starlings. Most garden birds likely to use boxes are passerines, i.e. of about the size of the sparrow, and a hole of $1\frac{1}{4}$ in. diameter is quite large enough. A hole this size will admit the tree sparrow, all the tit family, nuthatch, pied flycatcher and house martin. The wryneck requires a $1\frac{1}{2}$-in. diameter hole. The other potential users of a garden nesting box require larger entrances, e.g., redstart ($1\frac{1}{2}$–2 in.), sand martin (2 in.), swift ($2\frac{1}{2}$ in.), green woodpecker ($2\frac{1}{2}$–3 in.), and great spotted woodpecker (2–$2\frac{1}{2}$ in.). But, unfortunately, if suitable boxes are placed with holes 2 in. or larger in diameter, they will at once be seized by starlings.

An important dimension of every box is the overall depth. So often one sees boxes offered for sale which are so shallow that a cat or squirrel would find it very easy to reach the nest by thrusting its paw through the entrance hole. No box should be less than 9 in. from the entrance hole to the floor because one has to take into account the fact that some birds build quite thick foundations to their nests even in a box, reducing the effective depth by up to 2 in. or more. The floor area should not be less than 4 in. square for the passerines and 6 in. square for larger birds such as the woodpeckers.

Attracting Birds

The well-made nest box is far from unsightly and should not offend the eye of even the fussiest of gardeners. However, there are ways of disguising them. The first boxes I made I covered with silver-birch bark from a felled tree. The bark strips off very easily and the way I went about covering the boxes was as follows: after the wooden pieces for the sides, top and bottom had been cut to size, I cut pieces of bark slightly larger than each piece and stuck them on with *Bostik*. The bark does not lie absolutely flat, so I put all the wooden members, each with its piece of bark, into a vice, which I screwed up tight. After a couple of days, not only was the bark flattened but it was stuck hard to the wood. The boxes were then assembled with screws and, after nearly ten years are almost as good as new except at the edges where birds have torn the bark in their hunt for insects. Mounted on silver-birch trees these boxes are quite hard to distinguish from a distance.

Another type of box can be made from hollowed-out logs, but this is a tedious business. I have, however, made one or two from thick bark removed from oak logs bought for burning. When these have dried thoroughly the bark, which is about ¾ in. thick, strips off quite easily and is remarkably tough. The edges are trimmed straight so that they will butt properly and two pieces of bark glued together make a neat cylinder. The bottom of the cylinder is closed permanently by a circular piece of hardwood which fits inside the cylinder, glued in position with *Bostik* and the crevices, which are inevitable because the cylinder cannot have a perfectly smooth interior, are filled with plastic wood. The top of the box is levelled off and smoothed and a flat hardwood lid, hinged from the vertical batten attaching the box to a tree, is closed with two substantial catches, one on each side of the box. Both the lid and the bottom of the box can be made to match the rest of it in appearance by gluing on odd pieces of bark. This very home-made design may sound rather a jerry-built affair, but two of them have lasted three years and are used by tits. Examination in the autumn shows the interiors to be perfectly dry and snug even after an English summer. So far, unfortunately, I haven't been able to persuade nuthatches to use them.

Attracting Birds

Some small birds will nest in long tunnel-like affairs such as lengths of drainpipe, and swifts have been induced to nest in oblong boxes, at least 18 in. long with a small hole at one end, but, to attract swifts, such nest boxes have to be placed very high—too high for the ordinary garden bird photographer. Of course it is known that robins, tits and even flycatchers will build in old kettles and other receptacles wedged in suitable places, but for the small garden owner at any rate it is far more satisfactory to use properly-made boxes than to have his hedges and trees adorned with discarded kitchen utensils.

If entrance holes are accidentally made too large or are enlarged by, for example, squirrels, they can be partially blocked by nailing or screwing a piece of wood or metal across the bottom of the hole from the inside of the box.

The open-fronted type of box is popular with robins, spotted flycatchers, pied wagtails and redstarts. This is simply the ordinary type of nest box but with only half the front covered.

MATERIALS FOR NEST BOXES

Hardwood is by far the best material for nest-box construction because of its durability and ease of working, though other materials have been tried. Some boxes have been made of tin with the edges soldered, but the objection to this is the poor insulation and the possibility of condensation inside the box. Plastics have been used with success in Sweden, but this is hardly a material for the amateur.

As a rule nest boxes should be completely air- and water-tight, except for the entrance, but for some of the larger birds, such as the great spotted woodpecker, drainage holes in the bottom may be necessary to aid sanitation. All wooden boxes should be treated with some preservative before being fixed in position. Creosote is the cheapest and is very effective. I have used both this and *Cuprinol* which provides excellent protection and, being a green liquid, often matches the surroundings better than a creosoted box.

Many bird boxes one sees offered for sale are fitted with a small perch under the entrance hole. This is quite unnecessary and may even be dangerous because it may help a predator to gain a foot-hold. So far as photography is concerned, it will seldom be found that the bird uses the perch before entering the box to provide a pose for the camera. Most birds stop at the entrance hole itself to make sure that all is clear before entering the nest, offering a much more natural picture, and at the same time a better position to focus the camera upon because the position of the bird will be more exactly fixed than when it is sitting on a perch. A perch somewhere near the box, however, is often a good idea as anyone will have noticed who has watched flycatchers feeding young. Many birds like to make a short stop near the nest in a position which commands clear views in all directions, and if no natural lookout is available, the photographer can contrive one and use this for his pictures.

An excellent source of advice on the subject of nest boxes is the booklet, *Nestboxes*, by Edwin Cohen and Bruce Campbell, and published by the British Trust for Ornithology at 2s. 6d. This gives details of a number of specialized designs for different bird species, with full details of construction, materials to use, dimensions and so forth. If it is preferred to buy nest boxes, a very wide range of types and sizes is offered by Birdcraft Products, Green-rigg Works, Woodford Green, Essex. A hole-type nesting box is also made for the Royal Society for the Protection of Birds by Scottish war-blinded ex-servicemen (see Fig. 3).

PLACING THE NEST BOXES

When siting a box which, as a rule, should face in a northerly direction, i.e. in the arc between north-east and north-west, it is essential that it be securely fixed to its support. The supporting batten may be nailed or screwed to a tree or pole or, in the case of a wall, fixed by long wall nails. An alternative to nails or screws is the teak pin, which will not damage saws if the tree is ultimately to be felled. For fixing to hardwood trees, holes must first be bored with a brace and bit for these pins, but they can be driven into soft wood with a hammer. Alternatively, the boxes can be strapped or wired to trees, but such an arrangement is less sightly. In some cases the natural inclination of a tree may permit the nest box to be inclined forward, but if not a wedge-shaped piece of wood can be fixed between the box and the vertical batten. This wedge should be as narrow as possible to prevent moisture collecting along its top edge.

It will be found as a rule that birds do not like boxes hidden in dense cover because the shelter thus offered may also offer a hiding-place for enemies. Not only should birds be able to make unobstructed flights to the box but they prefer a site which has a clear view of the surroundings. Thus, boxes on trees bordering a lawn are much more likely to be used than if hidden in a hedge or close-growing tree. Even a box fixed to the top or side of a post standing isolated in a clear space is preferred to one which has been concealed in foliage.

Other Artificial Nesting Sites

Not all species will use boxes. Ledges or flat open boxes are popular with some birds, and empty coco-nut shells, old seed trays and similar objects, if fixed solidly in suitable sites, may be used. In all such cases, the containers should have a number of $\frac{1}{2}$-in. diameter holes drilled into the bases to provide drainage. No bird will use a receptacle which becomes waterlogged.

Tree-creepers, so I am told, will nest under pieces of bark fixed to a tree trunk. I haven't tried this because in my garden such a site would be too accessible to such predators as squirrels and cats, and it seems to me that an ordinary box of the type designed for tits would suit them. I have, however, never had tree-creepers nest in my garden, though they are often to be seen running up and down the trees in search of insects.

It is possible to attract some birds by providing a natural foundation upon which a nest can be built, and I have already mentioned the use to which worn birch brooms are put. Most species nesting in the open choose a fork in a tree or shrub as a support, and these can sometimes be contrived at a spot convenient for photography by tying small growing branches or twigs together to form a firm platform. Shrubs which do not have suitable 'forks', such as rhododendrons and hazels, are seldom chosen for nests and it is best to avoid making artificial sites in

Attracting Birds

them. In all cases of birds which do not use boxes the kind of situation they prefer should if possible be ascertained and then, if such places are not really provided by the trees and shrubs in the garden in positions suitable for photography, sites should be found and made to look as natural as possible.

Birds always appreciate their nesting boxes, baths and feeding devices so placed that they can reconnoitre the approaches from some commanding position. Any device intended to attract birds will only be used with reluctance if it is near anything which might give cover to an enemy. One has only to watch a bird feeding, say, for a few minutes to notice how it is always on the *qui vive*. It never appears to be free from apprehension. One should bear this in mind and place any of these devices in positions which will give the birds as much assurance as possible.

MATERIALS FOR NESTS

An examination of the nests of my garden birds will show what their needs are in the way of materials. Many of the larger birds, such as thrushes and blackbirds, use thin twigs for the foundation. There is generally a plentiful supply of these, especially where there are silver birches which shed twigs and small branches whenever there is a high wind. But the birds will appreciate help with the finer materials such as moss, hair, feathers and short lengths of wool of any colour but white. It is often advisable to provide materials to save plants in the garden. For example, both starlings and sparrows would tear lengths of aubretia from my rockery until I resorted to leaving small piles of rough grass cut from under the trees. When planting shrubs and young trees I tied them to stakes using narrow lengths of old carpet underfelt between tree and stake: the birds promptly tore the underfelt to pieces. Now I give them their own felt which I tuck into crevices in wattle hurdling. Some of the moss removed from the lawn with a springbok rake is, in the spring, left in small heaps under cover instead of being added to the compost heap. Hair combings are put into a small wooden box hung up under the eaves of the toolshed, and I have identified my grey hair in the nests of robins, chaffinches, dunnocks and willow warblers.

Attracting Birds

There is no limit to the number of bird boxes which may be erected in a garden, though it is most unlikely that they will all be used. It is important that they should not be too close together and essential that the entrance of one should not be visible from the front door of another, otherwise it is probable that neither will be occupied. I had, however, a somewhat unusual exception to this rule in my own garden. While a great tit was incubating in a box, a blackbird built a nest on top of it. When the tits were feeding their young, the blackbird was incubating her eggs. So far as I could make out, the birds were not on speaking terms.

The general rule is that the boxes should face north-west and the reason for this is that the sun should not shine directly into the hole. It is possible to vary this rule, however, if the entrance is screened from the direct rays of the sun by foliage. Of course, this foliage must be in place when the bird starts to build because she is not to know that the bare twigs and branches in front of the box will be clothed by the time of year when the sun becomes really hot. So far as height is concerned, the requirements of comfortable photography must be borne in mind, so an upper limit of about 5 ft. should be imposed. And, because box-nesters do not like to be too near the ground, the box should not be fixed lower than about 3 ft. 6 in. This is a very handy height when working from a hide.

CHAPTER 3

The Equipment

Whatever kind of bird photograph is being taken, the ideals to be aimed at are first, the recording of the finest possible feather detail, and secondly, accurate rendering of colour: but achieving the second without the first will not make a really good bird portrait. There is no excuse for producing fuzzy images or so-called 'soft-focus' effects because even with an inexpensive camera it is possible to make excellent pictures of critical definition. So far as colour rendering is concerned, the photographer should, to begin with, stick to the reversal or negative materials which have already given him good service, bearing in mind that with few exceptions our commonest garden birds are of sombre or delicate colouring, demanding a film which will capture the pastel shades of, for instance, a hen chaffinch's breast as well as the solid black displayed by a great tit.

As I have already said, this book makes no attempt to instruct the photographer who stalks wild birds in their natural haunts, but is strictly for the amateur who would like to make pictures in colour of the birds frequenting his garden. Most of these amateurs use the 35-mm. format for their colour work, unlike the wild-bird specialist who, mainly for technical reasons, prefers the larger sizes. The 35-mm. man must often expect to be criticized by the wild-bird photographer on the ground that his pictures tend to show too much bird and not enough of the subject's natural surroundings. My own efforts suffer from this very fault, if it is a fault. The user of the larger camera can obtain as big an image from a greater distance of the bird itself as is possible on 35 mm., but can at the same time record the bird's nest or other surroundings. This can also be done with 35-mm. material and, when the picture is projected on a screen or enlarged on paper it should be as good or maybe better than the contact print made from larger reversal or negative film, assuming equal technical achievement in both cases. Where colour is concerned, however, there is simply no choice for the majority of amateurs because few can afford a larger size than 35 mm.

ADVANTAGES OF 35-MM. FORMAT

On the other hand, for the perfect picture the 35-mm. camera does demand a higher degree of skill than the larger formats because there is no room for cropping: the bird must be placed exactly right for a satisfactory composition and no space at all can be wasted. One can, however, at less expense make a number of shots from which the best can be chosen and the rest if need be discarded. From the point of view of bird photography alone, the outstanding advantage of the 35-mm. camera is that it is the only really practicable instrument for photographing birds in flight. With the depths of field available with 35-mm., 45-mm. and 50-mm. lenses, shutter speeds of 1/1,000 sec. or even higher, and daylight colour film with a speed of ASA160, no other camera can approach the miniature in this branch of the hobby.

So far as photographing birds in flight is concerned a useful tip may be inserted here. On some cameras, the *Leica* for instance, the 7-ft. focusing mark is just about midway between infinity and the closest focusing point on the lens scale. Unless, therefore, the more or less exact distance at which a flying bird will pass before the camera is known, having the lens prefocused at 7 ft. will involve the minimum focusing movement for any distance on the focusing scale. If for any reason it proves impracticable to take an exposure reading from an object of similar colouring to that of the bird one is waiting for, an aperture of f/5·6 is the most useful with the shutter speed set to match.

There are other advantages of the 35-mm. size, which apply equally to all kinds of photography. For demonstrations, lectures or displays to clubs and societies the 35-mm. slide is unrivalled. It is less bulky, lighter and easier to handle than the larger sizes and, so far as definition on a projection screen is concerned, the

IV. *Great tit*. Same data as for the nuthatch (Plate III).

well-made 35-mm. transparency will stand comparison with any. The projectors, even those for covering long projection distances, are the cheapest available. In fact, a suitable projector and a large number of slides can be carried about in quite a small case and plugged into any light circuit, provided the voltage is suitable. A final advantage of the 2-in. (50-mm.) square slide is that it is less liable to breakage than the larger sizes.

VIEW-RANGEFINDER *v.* SINGLE-LENS REFLEX

If the bird photographer is new to the 35-mm. format he will find that the relative merits of the combined view- and range-finder and the single-lens reflex cameras are hotly disputed by established 35-mm. users. The deciding factor should be the purposes for which the camera is intended and if, as is generally the case, the camera will have to serve other photographic purposes as well as portraits of birds, he must choose that instrument which, all other things being equal, has the widest application.

Generally speaking, the view-rangefinder camera will be lighter than the single-lens reflex, its mechanism is simpler because there is no mirror to be moved out of the way before the shutter operates, and it is therefore quieter, a quality which may be important in bird photography; and lenses of comparable optical quality are sometimes cheaper.

The single-lens reflex should offer more accurate framing of the picture because the subject is composed and focused through the lens that takes the picture. This important advantage of the SLR is endorsed by some leading makers of the view-rangefinger designs who supply reflex focusing attachments for their cameras; and the reflex framing and focusing principle holds good whatever lens is being used.

There are disadvantages in both cameras, depending upon the user. Some find difficulty in 'coinciding' the images in a view-rangefinder camera, and others cannot see the entire picture in the viewfinder because, perhaps, their spectacles get in the way. Some people again cannot focus sharply on ground-glass screens, however excellent the quality of the screen. To help such people some camera-makers insert an optical split-image rangefinder in the centre of the ground-glass viewer. These work very well with lenses with a larger maximum opening than about f/5·6, or when the lens can be opened wide for viewing and then either manually or automatically closed down to the correct aperture for exposure.

It has already been pointed out that bird portraits must be sharply focused, but no amount of care in focusing will produce a sharp picture if there is any camera movement. Until the last two or three years few SLR cameras would produce as sharp an image as the best of the view-rangefinder types. By this I do not imply that the optical equipment of the SLR is inferior, but there is more movement in the SLR mechanism than there is in the view-rangefinder camera and this is borne out by the noise made by the two, though SLR instruments are today much quieter than they were. I think there can be little doubt that mirror movement in the SLR is responsible for some unsharpness unless high shutter speeds are used and the camera is very rigidly supported. Most of my own bird pictures have been taken with an *Exakta*, but I invariably use a very stout tripod and I have had no reason to complain of blurred feathers or other details.

CHOICE OF EQUIPMENT

So far as the following discussion of equipment for the garden bird photographer is concerned, like everyone else, I have my own preferences in the matter of 35-mm. cameras and lenses for this kind of work, but each man must decide for himself what he can afford. As I have said before, most of us can very well make do with what equipment we already have, with the addition perhaps of close-up portrait lenses or, if the camera is of the interchangeable-lens type, with telescopic lenses or those of long focal length. If the camera is suitable, a bellows in conjunction with the optical section of a long-focal-length lens, of 135 mm. say, is a most valuable tool for photographing birds from long distances to extreme close-ups. One thing can be assumed, however, and that is that all the instruments and materials I refer to are first-class products of well-established firms. Naturally some equipment is better suited than others for this absorbing branch of the hobby, but it must be realized that good results are often due as much

The Equipment

to the man taking the photograph as to his camera and lenses.

Most 35-mm. cameras will focus down to about one metre, but the principal object, the bird, which is not very large anyway, will form far too small an image for the resulting transparency or negative to constitute a portrait, though the camera with its normal lens of 45-mm. or 50-mm. focal length will do very well without any supplementary lenses or other equipment for photographing a nest on such a scale that the surroundings are included in the picture. Many 35-mm. reflex cameras will focus closer than one metre, but as a general rule all cameras require either supplementary lenses for fitting to the front of the normal lens or, in the case of those cameras which have full lens interchangeability, lenses of long focal length or of the telescopic variety can be inserted in the camera. It is, by the way, a mistake to refer to all long-focus lenses as 'telescopic' as these are of special construction.

SUPPLEMENTARY LENSES

The positive supplementary lens, fitted to the front of the camera lens, is the simplest aid to close-ups. Commonly known as 'portrait' lenses, they are available in a range of focal lengths, the standard being the 'dioptre'. A lens of 1 dioptre has a focal length of 1 metre, a 2-dioptre lens a focal length of 0·5 metre, and so on.

Most camera manufacturers offer special lenses for portraiture. The Kodak *Kodisk* is an example which, fitted to a camera of the simple fixed-focus fixed-aperture type, enables one to focus sharply on objects between 28 in. and 39½ in. If the camera has a focusing lens, pictures can be taken as close as 20 in. from the object. The data for all lens-subject distances are given in Table 1 of cameras scaled in feet or metres.

To fill the 1 × 1½-in. frame with a bird portrait, one is seldom likely to be nearer than about 2 ft. from the object, which means that the camera focus should be set at 5 ft. (see Table 1). These supplementaries fit over the camera lens, and for screw-in mounts the *Portra* lenses are available in three strengths: +1, +2 and +3. The data for the +1 *Portra* lens are identical with those in Table 1. With the +2 lens a subject can be focused as near as 12·5 in.

51

The Equipment

Table 1. Data for *Kodisk* Close-up Lenses

CAMERAS SCALED IN FEET

Camera focus setting	Lens-to-subject distance	Camera focus setting	Lens-to-subject distance
Infinity	39½ in.	9 ft.	29 in.
50 ft.	37 in.	8 ft.	28 in.
40 ft.	36 in.	7 ft.	27 in.
25 ft.	35 in.	6 ft.	25½ in.
18 ft.	33 in.	5 ft.	24 in.
15 ft.	32½ in.	4½ ft.	23 in.
12 ft.	31 in.	4 ft.	21½ in.
10 ft.	29½ in.	3 ft.	19 in.

CAMERAS SCALED IN METRES

Camera focus setting	Lens-to-subject distance	Camera focus setting	Lens-to-subject distance
Infinity	100 cm.	3·0 m.	75 cm.
20 m.	97 cm.	2·5 m	70 cm.
15 m.	94 cm.	2·0 m.	66 cm.
10 m.	92 cm.	1·75 m.	63 cm.
7 m.	89 cm.	1·5 m.	61 cm.
5 m.	84 cm.	1·25 m.	56 cm.
4 m.	80 cm.	1·0 m.	50 cm.

(33 cm. on cameras with metre scales); and with the +3 lens the camera can be brought as near as 9·5 in. (25 cm. on cameras scaled in metres), but only very seldom is one likely to be taking pictures at such close ranges. In all cases, the lens should be stopped down to at least f/8 to obtain satisfactory depth of field.

The range of Kodak N supplementary lenses extends the scope of the *Retina* 1b, 11c, 111c and *Retinette* cameras to cover all aspects of bird photography. These supplementaries screw into the front thread of the standard lens. Of the various N lenses available, the one most useful to the bird photographer is the N1, with which he can approach his quarry as close as 17¾ in. Data for this lens are given in Table 2. The object distance is measured,

52

The Equipment

not from the front of the supplementary lens as is usual with the simple types already referred to earlier, but from the film plane, which corresponds approximately to the rear upper edge of the chromium-plated camera top. The figures for field size are most useful because it enables one to gauge roughly beforehand how far away from the target a hide should be set before the final focusing is done. The last column refers to the scale of the image, i.e. at the closest object distance (17¾ in.), the bird will appear on the film in the proportion of 1 : 7·4, or a little more than one-seventh life-size.

According to Table 2, a camera-object distance of 30 in. would cover a large enough area to include, say, a great spotted woodpecker and part of his surroundings though, with very careful positioning of the camera and provided the bird would oblige, the area at a camera-object distance of 19¾ in. would yield a real close-up. Such a view would of necessity have to be a profile because the depth of field, except at f/16 and smaller, is too shallow for other aspects of the bird.

CLOSE-UP RANGEFINDER

A useful accessory for making pictures with the N1 supplementary lens is a close-up rangefinder. This shows the exact field of view and automatic parallax compensation ensures that the finder view always corresponds to the image recorded on the film. This rangefinder is made in two models, one for cameras with 50-mm. lenses and the other for cameras with 45-mm. lenses. Full instructions are issued with the rangefinder, but the following practice will simplify setting-up the camera when pre-focusing on a nest or perch: screw the supplementary lens into the front of the camera lens and set the focusing scale of the camera and the focusing disc of the close-up rangefinder to the same distance figure, which can be determined from Table 2. Now look through the close-up rangefinder and approach the subject until the two images in the rangefinder field fuse into one. At exactly this spot should the camera be set ready for the bird.

For their 50-mm. f/2·8 *Tessar* lenses, Zeiss make a series of

Table 2. N1 Data for 50-mm. Lenses

Approx. field size (inches) RETINA III C	*Approx. field size (inches)* REFLEX S, RETINA III S, I B, RETINETTE I A	*Object distance (inches)*	*Camera setting (feet)*	*f/5·6* f	*f/5·6* b	*f/8* f	*f/8* b	*f/11* f	*f/11* b	*f/16* f	*f/16* b	*f/22* f	*f/22* b	*Image ratio*
				Sharp zone (inches) in front of (f) and behind (b) the object plane at apertures shown										
17 1/2 × 26 3/8	15 3/4 × 23 3/8	38 1/4	INF	34 5/8	43	33 1/4	45 1/4	31 3/4	48 1/2	29 1/2	54 3/4	27 1/2	66 1/2	1 : 18
16 5/8 × 24 3/4	15 1/8 × 22 3/4	35 3/4	50	33 1/8	40 7/8	31 3/4	42 1/2	30 3/8	45 1/2	28 5/8	51 1/4	26 1/4	60	1 : 17·5
14 5/8 × 22	13 3/8 × 20 1/8	32 3/8	15	29 3/4	35 1/8	28 3/4	37 1/4	27 1/2	39 3/8	26	43 1/4	24	50	1 : 15
13 1/4 × 19 7/8	12 1/8 × 18 1/4	30	10	27 5/8	32 3/8	26 3/4	33 7/8	25 3/4	35 7/8	24 1/2	38 3/4	22 3/4	44	1 : 13·3
10 5/8 × 16	9 3/4 × 14 1/2	24 3/4	5	23 1/4	26 3/8	22 5/8	27 1/4	21 7/8	28 1/8	20 7/8	30	19 3/4	33	1 : 10·8
8 1/8 × 12 1/4	7 3/8 × 11 1/4	19 3/4	3	18 7/8	20	18 1/2	21 3/8	18	22	17 1/4	22 1/2	16 1/2	24	1 : 8·1
7 1/2 × 11 1/4	6 5/8 × 10	17 3/4	2·5	17	18 1/2	16 3/4	18 7/8	16 1/2	19 3/8	16	20 1/8	15 1/2	21 1/8	1 : 7·4

Table 3. Data for 1-m. *Proxar* with *Tessar* 50-mm. f/2·8 Lens

Field size	*Camera to object distance*	*Camera setting*	*Depth of field at f/8*	*Depth of field at f/16*	*Image ratio*
1 ft. 5 1/4 in. × 2 ft. 2 1/4 in.	4 ft 1/2 in.	Infinity	3 ft. 5 1/2 in. — 4 ft. 7 1/2 in.	3 ft. 1 in. — 5 ft. 7 in.	1 : 19
1 ft. 3/4 in. × 1 ft. 7 1/2 in.	2 ft. 11 1/2 in.	10 ft.	2 ft. 8 in. — 3 ft. 3 1/2 in.	2 ft. 5 in. — 3 ft. 9 in.	1 : 14·1
10 1/4 in. × 1 ft. 3 1/2 in.	2 ft. 4 in.	5 ft.	2 ft. 2 in. — 2 ft. 7 in.	2 ft. — 2 ft. 10 in.	1 : 11·4
7 1/2 in. × 11 1/2 in.	1 ft. 10 in.	3 ft.	1 ft. 8 1/2 in. — 1 ft. 11 1/2 in.	1 ft. 7 1/2 in. — 2 ft. 1 in.	1 : 8·4
6 3/4 in. × 10 1/4 in.	1 ft. 7 1/2 in.	2 ft. 6 in.	1 ft. 6 1/2 in. — 1 ft. 8 1/2 in.	1 ft. 5 1/2 in. — 1 ft. 10 in.	1 : 7·5

The Equipment

Proxar lenses of various focal lengths. Of these the first two, with focal lengths of 1m. and 0·5m., are likely to be the most useful to the owner of a *Contaflex*, for example. With the 1-m. *Proxar* it is possible to set the camera as near as 1 ft. 4 in. from the target to take in a field of $6\frac{3}{4} \times 10\frac{1}{4}$ in. to secure an image a little larger than one-seventh life-size. With the 0·5-m. *Proxar* one can obtain a larger image of a smaller field. The exact figures for the 1-m. *Proxar* are given in Table 3. If these *Proxars* are used on the *Contaflex*, which is a single-lens reflex camera, the parallax-free viewfinder will show the exact field covered and the camera can be focused in the usual way. The subject distance should be measured from the front rim of the supplementary lens, and an aperture of f/8 should give adequate depth of field if the subject distance is not too short, but if flash is the light source the aperture can generally be closed down still further with advantage.

SPECIAL CLOSE-UP ACCESORIES

Owners of *Contax* models 11, 11a, 111 and 111a will find the *Contameter* a useful device for close-up work. This consists of a combined range- and viewfinder with three Zeiss *Proxar* supplementary lenses, which fit all the 50-mm. *Contax* lenses except the collapsible f/3·5 *Tessar*. Except for extreme close-ups, the most useful *Proxar* for the *Contameter* is the '50', with which it is possible to obtain an image ratio of 1 : 10 with a field of $7\frac{7}{16}$ in. $\times$ 1 ft. $2\frac{5}{32}$ in. at a working distance of 1 ft. $7\frac{3}{4}$ in. The greatest depth of field, enough for a profile view of a small bird, is $3\frac{1}{4} - 5\frac{1}{32}$ in. at f/22.

An optical near-focusing device is made for all *Leica* models up to 111g. The focusing mount of this device screws into the lens ring on the camera and is fitted with a wedge prism which positions itself in front of the rangefinder opening and thereby permits critical focusing at short distances. It also includes a field diaphragm to compensate for parallax as well as the reduced field. This focusing mount has a bayonet for locking the tube of the *Leica* 50-mm. lens in position. With this device distances between $3\frac{1}{2}$ ft. and $16\frac{1}{2}$ in., measured from the film plane, are focusable with the built-in *Leica* rangefinder, giving image sizes of 1 : 17·5

55

The Equipment

up to 1 : 6·5. The field size varies from 1 ft. 5 in. × 2 ft. 1 in. down to as small as $5\frac{3}{4}$ × $8\frac{1}{2}$ in., which is close enough to yield a large portrait of any of the smaller birds. With the 50-mm. *Summicron* the largest image size is 1 : 8 with a field size of $7\frac{5}{8}$ × $11\frac{3}{8}$ in. Data for this device are shown in Table 4.

Table 4. Data for the Leitz Near-focusing Device

Field size	Range of depth of field $f/8$	$f/16$	Image ratio
1 ft. $4\frac{1}{2}$ in. × 2 ft. $\frac{3}{4}$ in.	$6\frac{3}{4}$ in.	$13\frac{1}{2}$ in.	1 : 17·5
1 ft. 2 in. × 1 ft. $9\frac{1}{4}$ in.	5 in.	10 in.	1 : 15
$11\frac{1}{4}$ in. × 1 ft. 5 in.	$3\frac{1}{4}$ in.	$6\frac{1}{2}$ in.	1 : 12
$8\frac{1}{4}$ in. × 1 ft. $0\frac{3}{4}$ in.	$1\frac{3}{4}$ in.	$3\frac{3}{4}$ in.	1 : 9
7 in. × $10\frac{1}{2}$ in.	$1\frac{1}{4}$ in.	$2\frac{3}{4}$ in.	1 : 7·5
6 in. × $9\frac{1}{4}$ in.	1 in.	2 in.	1 : 6·5

A similar device is made for the *Leica* M cameras which gives image scales from 1 : 15 up to 1 : 7·5. This is fitted to the camera like an interchangeable lens, the automatic parallax adjustment acting as with the ordinary interchangeable lenses, and the image reduction is corrected accordingly. For the 111g *Leica* a close-up supplementary screws into the front of any *Leica* lens with a front diameter of 42 mm. An auxiliary unit clamps on to the camera, with the aid of which objects between $34\frac{5}{8}$ in. and $20\frac{3}{4}$ in. can be focused through the standard built-in range- and viewfinder, the automatic parallax compensation of the finder remaining fully effective. The area coverable ranges from $14\frac{1}{2}$ × $20\frac{3}{4}$ in. down to $7\frac{7}{8}$ × $11\frac{3}{4}$ in., the image ratios obtainable being from 1 : 15·4 up to 1 : 8·3.

Another Leitz close-up aid is the dual-range 50-mm. f/2 *Summicron*. This lens can be used for the normal range of infinity down to 1 m. and also for 88 cm. to 48 cm. ($34\frac{1}{2}$ in. to 19 in.).

56

The Equipment

For the close-up range an optical viewfinder attachment is pushed on to the lens whereby the coupled measuring viewfinder can be used for close-up subjects. Image ratios from 1 : 15 up to 1 : 7·5 are obtainable in this way and, as with all devices of this nature, the lens should be stopped down to f/8 or less for close-up subjects.

INTERCHANGEABLE LENS COMPONENTS

Intermediate devices between the supplementary lenses of the 'portrait' type and objectives of long focal length are interchangeable front lens components which can be used with some cameras. For example, by substituting a 5-element component for the standard front element in the *Contaflex*, it is possible to convert the 50-mm. lens to one of 85-mm. focal length. Such a combination is very useful for photographing, for example, a bird feeding young in the nest because of the larger image obtained of the bird itself from the same working distance as with the 50-mm. lens, the ratio being 1·7 (i.e. 85 ÷ 50) or nearly $1\frac{3}{4}$ times as big as the image secured with the 50-mm. lens. It is possible to focus on an object down to 6 ft. with the 85-mm. combination, at which distance the depth of field is 5 ft. $6\frac{1}{4}$ in. to 6 ft. $7\frac{1}{4}$ in. at f/8.

Another device for the *Contaflex* is the Zeiss 8 × 30B monocular. When screwed into the front of the 50-mm. *Tessar* the focal length of the combination becomes 8 × 50, or 400 mm., giving an image eight times the size of that obtained with the 50-mm. lens. As the front glass diameter of the monocular is 30 mm., as shown by the designation 8 × 30, the effective aperture of the combination becomes 400 ÷ 30, or about f/14. As users of split-image rangefinders will appreciate, one section of the finder will 'blackout' so only the surrounding focusing screen can be used. With this monocular an image ratio of 1 : 17 can be had from a distance of 26 ft. with a depth of field from just over 25 ft. to just under 27 ft. It is possible to secure larger image ratios, of course, even up to nearly half life-size from a distance of 7 ft., but the depth of field is almost negligible. As with all lenses of long focal length, the slightest camera movement during exposure will blur the picture so that, unless conditions permit an exposure of 1/250

The Equipment

sec. or faster, a sturdy tripod is essential. Owners of the *Contaflex* models I and II who contemplate using this Zeiss monocular should first of all consult either the manufacturers of the camera or their agents. The reason for this is that the front lens mounts of these cameras were never designed to support the leverage arising from attaching the monocular and damage to the front lens cell is possible.

Long Focal-length Lenses

For the owner of a camera which will accept fully-interchangeable lenses, there is an almost bewildering range of optical equipment. Here again he must buy the best he can afford, though naturally the product of a firm of world-wide reputation will give him the best results in bird portraiture as in other applications of the camera.

It would not be possible to give a complete list of the lenses of longer than normal focal length, i.e. 45 mm., 50 mm. and 58 mm., but two simple diagrams are given in Fig. 4 which show roughly the field of view from the same camera position offered by lenses of different focal lengths in one sketch (Fig. 4A) and, in the other, how the same field can be covered from greater camera-subject distances with lenses of longer focal length (Fig. 4B). A few general observations may be made, however, on some of the most useful long lenses.

An optic of 85 mm. is a very useful aid in bird portraiture, though such lenses are rather costly. Table 5, for instance, gives the principal data for the *Sonnar* 85-mm. f/2 lens, which is designed for portraiture with the *Contarex*. A faster lens of the same focal length is the Leitz f/1·5 *Summarex*. The angle of view of this lens is 28 deg., i.e. only 1 deg. wider than lenses of 90-mm. focal length, which are in the main much cheaper. The advantage of a maximum aperture of f/1·5 is found, however, when the light is inadequate for smaller lens openings.

The most popular lens of longer than normal focal length is the 90 mm., made by most leading manufacturers. Most lenses of this type are speeded at f/4, though there are faster lenses in this focal length, examples being the f/2 *Summicron*, the f/2·5 *Angenieux*,

58

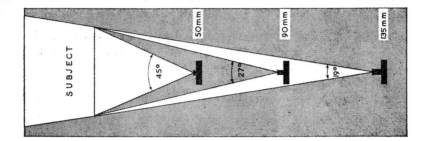

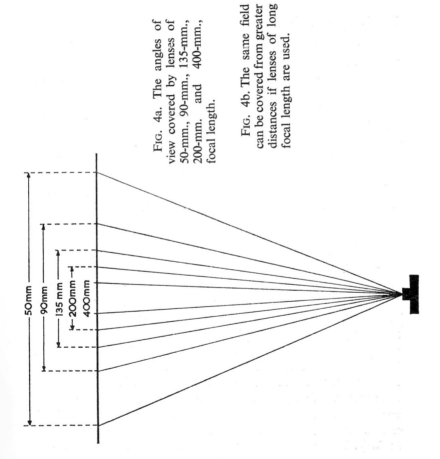

Fig. 4a. The angles of view covered by lenses of 50-mm., 90-mm., 135-mm., 200-mm. and 400-mm. focal length.

Fig. 4b. The same field can be covered from greater distances if lenses of long focal length are used.

the f/2·8 *Elmarit* and others. The 90-mm. lenses give an image size of 1 4/5 times that yielded by a 50-mm. lens from the same camera-subject distance, and the 100-mm. or 105-mm. lens, of which there are again many types of various speeds, yields an image twice the size of the standard camera lens. Many of these lenses can be used direct on the camera in their own focusing mounts though, when the optical section only is mounted on a bellows, which is in turn attached to the camera and acts as a focusing mount, their scope is greatly widened.

THE POPULAR 135-MM. LENS

The next commonest step-up in focal length is the 135 mm., which is gradually becoming one of the most popular for many classes of work, including bird portraits. Yielding an image of about 2 3/5 the size given by the 50-mm. lens, the 135-mm. optic is as a rule of f/4 or f/4·5 and the definition of the best-known varieties, even when wide open, leaves nothing to be desired. One of my favourite lenses for large birds is a 135-mm. f/4 *Sonnar*, originally made for a *Contax*, but fitted with an adaptor for the *Exakta*. The main data for the 135-mm. f/4 *Sonnar* are as shown in Table 6. Lenses in the 150-mm. and 180-mm. focal lengths come next in order and are made for several SLR cameras.

LENSES OF 200-MM. AND OVER

Of the lenses with a focus of 200 mm. and over, outstanding examples are the 200-mm. f/4 *Telyt*, made for the *Visoflex* I and II with reflex focusing, the 250-mm. *Sonnar* for the *Contaflex* (see Table 7), and the series of 'follow-focus' *Novoflex* lenses with pistol grips. These are made in four focal lengths for 35-mm. namely, 240-mm. f/4·5, 300-mm. f/5·6, 400-mm. f/5·6 and 640-mm. f/9, all with the designation *Noflexar*. The image sizes as compared with the normal camera lens are arrived at in the usual way by dividing the focal length of the long lens by that of the standard camera lens. The *Noflexars* are made for most of the SLR cameras and for some of the view-rangefinder types. The 400-mm. f/5 *Telyt* is another lens of telephoto construction for use with

Table 5. Data for 85-mm. f/2 *Sonnar*

Field size	*Lens focused at*	*Depth of field* *f/4*	*f/8*	*f/16*	*Image ratio*
2 ft. 7 in. × 3 ft 11 in.	10 ft.	9 ft. 6 in. — 10 ft. 6 in.	9 ft. 1 in. — 11 ft. 2 in.	8 ft. 3 in. — 12 ft. 8 in.	1 : 34
1 ft. 6 in. × 2 ft. 3 in.	6 ft.	5 ft. 10 in. — 6 ft. 2 in.	5 ft. 8 in. — 6 ft. 4 in.	5 ft. 5 in. — 6 ft. 9 in.	1 : 20
11 in. × 1 ft. 5 in.	4 ft.	3 ft. 1 in. — 4 ft. 1 in.	3 ft. 10 in. — 4 ft. 1 in.	3 ft. 8 in. — 4 ft. 4 in.	1 : 12
6¼ in. × 9½ in.	2 ft. 6 in.	2 ft. 5¾ in. — 2 ft. 6¼ in.	2 ft. 5½ in. — 2 ft. 6½ in.	2 ft. 5 in. — 2 ft. 7 in.	1 : 7

Table 6. Data for 135-mm. f/4 *Sonnar*

Field size	*Lens focused at*	*Depth of field* *f/4*	*f/8*	*f/16*	*Image ratio*
2 ft. 5 in. × 3 ft. 9 in.	15 ft.	14 ft. 7 in. — 15 ft. 6 in.	14 ft. 2 in. — 16 ft.	13 ft. 5 in. — 17 ft. 1 in.	1 : 32
1 ft. 3 in. × 1 ft. 10 in.	8 ft.	7 ft. 10 in.— 8 ft. 1 in.	7 ft. 9 in. — 8 ft. 3 in.	7 ft. 7 in. — 8 ft. 6 in.	1 : 16
10½ in. × 1 ft. 3¾ in.	6 ft.	6 ft. — 6 ft. ¾ in.	5 ft. 1 in. — 6 ft. 1 in.	5 ft. 9 in. — 6 ft. 3 in.	1 : 11
8¼ in. × 1 ft. ½ in.	5 ft.	5 ft. — 5 ft. ½ in.	4 ft. 11 in. — 5 ft. 1 in.	4 ft. 10 in. — 5 ft. 2 in.	1 : 9

Table 7. Data for 250-mm. f/4 *Sonnar*

Field size	*Lens focused at*	*Depth of field* *f/4*	*f/8*	*f/16*	*Image ratio*
2 ft. 7 in. × 3 ft. 11 in.	30 ft.	29 ft. 6 in. — 30 ft. 6 in.	28 ft. 11 in. — 31 ft. 1 in.	28 ft. — 32 ft.	1 : 34
1 ft. 8 in. × 2 ft. 7 in.	20 ft.	19 ft. 9 in. — 20 ft. 2 in.	19 ft. 7 in. — 20 ft. 5 in.	19 ft. 1 in. — 20 ft. 11 in.	1 : 22
11½ in. × 1 ft. 5 in.	12 ft.	11 ft. 11 in. — 12 ft. ⅞ in.	11 ft. 10 in. — 12 ft. 2 in.	11 ft. 8 in. — 12 ft. 3 in.	1 : 12·5
8 in. × 1 ft.	9 ft.	8 ft. 11½ in. — 9 ft. ½ in.	8 ft. 11 in. — 9 ft. 1 in.	8 ft. 10 in. — 9 ft. 1 in.	1 : 9

Note. These lenses have other stops than those for which the figures are listed, and there are also intermediate settings. The above data however should serve as a guide.

either of the *Visoflex* reflex focusing attachments for the *Leica*. There are of course lenses of even longer focal lengths than those above and, while they find a use in photographing wild life, they would, I think, be an unnecessary extravagance for the garden bird photographer. The problems involved in their use, even if they could be afforded, also make sharp definition extremely difficult except in the most favourable circumstances.

A new lens for the *Contarex* is the Zeiss f/4·5 500-mm. telephoto which, being of the mirror type, has the important advantage of relatively short length. The definition is said to be excellent and the lens can be focused down to about 21 ft. 3 in. There is no iris, of course, but this is no disadvantage because with a lens of this focal length it is unnecessary to stop down to improve definition. In addition to the use of the shutter speeds, exposure times can if necessary be controlled by the use of neutral filters, though this would not often be necessary when using colour film. The lens is focused in the customary way in the camera viewfinder.

VALUE OF LONG-FOCUS LENSES

Most 35-mm. cameras when originally bought are fitted with lenses of 50 mm. or thereabouts, but the amateur who intends to use his camera for photographing birds in the garden will soon find that the lenses of longer focus are invaluable, even for casual snapshots of flocks of birds feeding on the lawn, bathing or going about their everyday tasks, while for prefocusing on a bait the longer lenses are all one could desire. For this kind of photography the 90-mm. or 105-mm. lens was a few years ago one of the most popular, either in its own mount or with the optical section fitted to focusing bellows. Today the 135-mm. lens seems to be ousting the 90 mm. The 135 mm., when fairly wide open and used at short camera-subject distances, will isolate a large bird or a smaller one on the nest from its surroundings, throwing it into sharp outline by suppressing the background. If the photographer takes up his position farther away from the bird, the effect is to flatten perspective, bringing the background closer to the subject and having all in focus. An example is a nest with surrounding foliage both equally sharp to indicate a natural nesting site.

The Equipment

Many 35-mm. users today habitually employ either a 180-mm. or a 200-mm. lens with which the photographer can isolate one or two birds from a group or snap a large bird, such as a jay or magpie, which has been attracted near a hide. The new lens glasses permit thinner and therefore lighter lens components and the modern light but strong alloys have meant less bulky mounts, with the result that reflex cameras and reflex housings for rangefinder cameras can sometimes be used hand-held at speeds down to 1/25 sec.

TRIPODS SHOULD BE USED

Hand-holding cameras with lenses longer than 200 mm. rarely gives satisfactory results with bird portraiture. The one exception is perhaps when photographing a bird in flight, where with fast film one can take a picture which, while not yielding much fine detail, will show characteristic flight attitudes, assuming of course that one is photographing a slow-flying bird and not trying to capture a kingfisher moving over the water at high speed. To obtain sharp definition, any lens should strictly speaking be mounted on a tripod and I have often imagined the kind of fun one could have during nesting time with, say, a 300-mm. or 400-mm. lens on a quick-moving pan-and-tilt head. Posted in a strategic position and not necessarily in a hide, with fast film and wide-open lens one could pick out birds in the garden—a blackbird or thrush tugging at a worm, parents feeding their young on the lawn, courtship and 'threat' displays and a host of interesting activities. A 20-exposure roll of High-speed *Ektachrome* or Super *Anscochrome* (if it could be obtained) would be used up in no time.

There are reasons other than an unsteady hand why really long lenses should be tripod-mounted. It will be obvious that the longer the lens the more will any camera movement be evident in the negative or transparency. With very long lenses, say 1,000 mm. and more, the faintest breeze will cause enough movement of the equipment to spoil the picture; and on warm days haze and air turbulence, invisible to the naked eye, may ruin the picture.

The Equipment

Depth of field figures quoted for lenses at different apertures are based on the diameter of the circle of confusion, which means, in short, the degrees of fuzziness acceptable in the finished picture. So far as the bird photographer is concerned, however, factors governing the depth of field are the focal length of the lens, the aperture in use and the distance between the lens and the object. A lens of long focal length at large aperture has a very shallow depth of field, while the greatest depth of field is obtained with a short-focus lens at a small aperture.

In bird photography, especially with the 35-mm. camera, where it is necessary for the best results to fill the frame with the subject, the depth of field problem becomes critical because we are working at short camera-object distances. The problem is to a large extent simplified if we are photographing the profile of a bird, even at a relatively large image scale. Obviously it is easier to obtain a picture of satisfactory overall sharpness if the long axis of the bird is at right angles to the lens-object axis. Even in such a case, however, we need a depth of field of 1 in. or so to ensure that both the head and wing are in sharp focus even on a small bird. It will thus be seen that a close-up of a bird presenting a three-quarter view to the lens could not possibly be sharp at a large image scale because if the head were in focus the tail would be blurred.

The depth of field of long-focal length and telescopic lenses is very shallow indeed, especially at relatively short distances and many pictures of birds sitting or feeding young which might otherwise have been good have been spoilt by the fact that while the bird and its nest have been sharp, objects in front of and behind the subject have been out of focus. An out-of-focus background is not objectionable if it doesn't include large fuzzy highlights, but an unsharp foreground will always spoil a picture. When these long lenses are used, they must be stopped down to the point where the picture is in focus from as near the lowest edge of the frame as possible up to and including the bird itself. If the viewpoint is high the problem is much simplified because the difference in distance from the lens to the bird and its immediate foreground

The Equipment

will not be so great as when a low viewpoint is chosen. If definition falls off behind the nest this is of small importance and may even make a better picture. This is where depth of field scales are valuable. If they are not engraved on the lens mount they should be noted in a pocket book. It is also an advantage to know something about the hyperfocal distances for the lenses used.

EXTENSION TUBES

A most useful and reasonably-priced accessory for the 35-mm. user is a set of extension tubes. Though intended mainly for photography in the very close ranges, i.e. up to an image ratio of 1 : 1 and even larger, tubes or rings can be serviceable for medium-range close-ups, as in the photography of birds when it is desired to capture a larger image than that obtainable with the normal camera lens of 50-mm. focal length.

The theory behind the increase of image ratio with extension tubes is quite simple. In accordance with optical laws the image distance, i.e. the distance between the lens and the plane of the film, must be increased when the subject distance, or the distance between the lens and subject, is decreased. Thus, when focusing on a subject close to the camera, the distance between the lens and the film plane must be longer than can be obtained by the normal focusing mount of the lens. To achieve this increase, extension rings or tubes can be inserted between the camera and the lens. One end of the ring or tube is screwed or bayoneted into the camera, and the lens is mounted at the other end of the tube.

One of the first accessories added to my *Exakta* was a set of these tubes and they have served me very well in close-up work. The set consists of five units, which can be used in various combinations to give 12 extension increases from 5 mm. to 60 mm. Naturally, the image scale obtainable with any increase in extension depends upon the focal length of the lens used in the set-up, and the data for lenses of 50 mm., 58 mm., 100 mm. and 135 mm. are given in Table 8. Not all the available data is included because it is unlikely that any bird photographer would take a picture life-size, for instance, which is the scale available with a tube extension of 50 mm. with a 50-mm. lens to give a lens-film distance of

The Equipment

100 mm. As an example of what can be done with these rings, I use two of them to give a 15-mm. extension on my 135-mm. *Sonnar*. With the camera fixed at 4 ft. 6 in. from the great spotted woodpecker bait, a field of view of just over 8 × 12 in. is covered, i.e. large enough to include the bird and a very little of his surroundings. As will be seen from Table 8, the image scale is 1 : 9, that is to say, the image of the great spotted woodpecker is about 1 in. long on the film, which is as large as one can safely accommodate on the long axis of the 24 × 36-mm. frame. The exposure factor shown in the table is 1·2, which means a proportionately longer exposure time than that calculated for the 135-mm. focal length. The reasons for this are explained towards the end of this chapter, but the exposure factors are included in Table 8 so as to keep all the relevant data together. I might mention here, however, that when exposure factors have to be taken into account, it is often much simpler to make the adjustment to the lens aperture than to juggle with shutter speeds. When using flash, particularly, it is far better to ascertain the correct speed for your shutter and to leave this undisturbed throughout a session. All this, too, is explained later on and examples are given to show the easiest way to go about the necessary calculations.

Reflex Attachments

The single-lens reflex camera is the ideal instrument for bird photography in the close-up ranges, but owners of many types of view-rangefinder cameras can adapt them to the reflex principle by using one of the attachments incorporating a mirror and a viewer, a combination which is obviously most useful with lenses of long focal length. One of these attachments is the *Novoflex* which can be used on the *Contax* IIa and IIIa, among other view-rangefinder cameras. Mirror reflex units and focusing bellows are produced by Zeiss for the *Contax* cameras, IIa and IIIa, and the owner of one of these cameras will find the *Panflex* reflex attachment a most useful accessory in photography of small birds. For this reflex unit Zeiss have developed the f/3·5 115-mm. *Panflex-Tessar* which, when fitted direct to the *Panflex* without a bellows, can be focused from infinity down to 3 ft. 10 in., when it will give

Table 8. Data for Extension Tubes with 50-mm., 58-mm., 100-mm. and 135-mm. Lenses

50-mm. Lens

Extension increase mm.	*Subject distance*	*Field size inches*	*Image ratio*	*Exposure increase factor*
5	1 ft. 9½ in.	9½ × 14	1 : 10	1·2
10	11¾ in.	4¾ × 7	1 : 2	1·4
58-mm. Lens				
5	2 ft. 4¾ in.	10½ × 15¾	1 : 11	1·2
10	15½ in.	5½ × 8¼	1 : 6	1·4
15	11 in.	3½ × 5½	1 : 4	1·6
100-mm. Lens				
5	6 ft. 10½ in.	18¾ × 28¼	1 : 20	1·1
10	3 ft. 7¼ in.	9½ × 14	1 : 10	1·2
15	2 ft 6 in.	6¼ × 9½	1 : 6	1·3
20	1 ft. 11½ in.	4¾ × 7	1 : 5	1·4
25	19¾ in.	3¾ × 5½	1 : 4	1·6
135-mm. Lens				
5	12 ft 4¾ in.	23½ × 35½	1 : 25	1·1
10	6 ft. 5 in.	13½ × 20¼	1 : 14	1·2
15	4 ft. 5 in.	8½ × 12¾	1 : 9	1·2
20	3 ft. 6 in.	6¼ × 9½	1 : 6	1·3
25	3 ft 10 in.	5 × 7½	1 : 5	1·4
30	3 ft. 5¼ in.	4¼ × 6½	1 : 4	1·5

The Equipment

an image scale of 1 : 8. If bellows are interposed between the *Panflex* and the lens, the focusing range is continuously increased to an image scale of 1 : 1. A scale of 1 : 8 is, however, quite large enough even for close-up bird portraits, because it means that if a picture were taken of a song thrush, say, and the entire bird appeared on the film, the actual image would be very slightly over 1 in. long. If all else were well done, focusing, exposure and so on, such an image when projected on a screen would yield a most striking picture.

Two models of the Leitz reflex housing, *Visoflex* I and II, are available for the *Leica*. The reflex housing is fitted to the camera in the same way as a lens, and two versions are made, one for screw-threaded lens flanges and the other for bayonet-mount models. The image is focused through an adjustable magnifier of × 5 on a fine-grained ground-glass screen, which has a circular mark on which the magnifier should be focused before focusing the subject. The magnifier can also be adjusted for minor faults in vision. When using a tripod, this should be screwed into the tripod bush of the reflex housing. Both upright and horizontal formats can be obtained by pressing a button and turning the camera at the same time. Various Leitz lenses can be used in the *Visoflex* I and both the *Telyt* 200-mm. and 400-mm. lenses are calibrated for this housing.

The *Visoflex* II is an improvement on the *Visoflex* I in that it is more compact so that it is possible to use the full focusing range from infinity to close-ups with lenses of 65-mm. focal length and longer. The single exception is the collapsible version of the 90-mm. *Elmar*. Two magnifying eyepieces are available, a pentaprism type of × 4 magnification which shows the image right way up and right way round, and a × 5 magnifier which presents an image right way up but laterally reversed. Any *Leica* user who owns lenses of 65-mm. focal length and upward will find the *Visoflex* II with the appropriate intermediate mounts or focusing threads most useful for bird close-ups. Lenses of shorter focal length than 65 mm. are not really suitable for the *Visoflex* II because the reflex housing is in effect an extension tube and 35-mm. and 50-mm. lenses could only be used for taking extreme close-ups of small objects where a very shallow depth of field is required. A summary of the fields

68

HOLE IN BARK
FOR BAIT →

1. Equipment set-up using the type of hide described on p. 87 and illustrated in Fig. 7. The cloth has been removed to show the arrangement of camera and flash. The auxiliary flash head to illuminate the bird's back is to the left of the picture. Also shown are the cheese tin (see p. 33) and two peanut holders (see p. 36), one in front of the tree and the other to the right. The camera is set for photographing a bird at the bait in the position indicated. The shutter is fired from indoors by a long pneumatic release.

The Equipment

covered, image ratios and other data for the various Leitz lenses
when used with the *Visoflex* II are given in Table 9.

Table 9. Data for *Visoflex* II for Three Useful Image Ratios

Image ratio	Field size (inch)	Depth of field (inch) f/5·6 f/8 f/11 f/16	Exposure increase factor
0·1 = 1 : 10	9·448 × 14·173	1·618 2·311 3·177 4·618	1·2
0·2 = 1 : 5	4·724 × 7·086	0·441 0·630 0·866 1·260	1·5
0·3 = 1 : 3	3·149 × 4·724	0·213 0·303 0·417 0·606	1·7

FOCUSING BELLOWS

For the 35-mm. photographer who wishes to get really close to
an individual bird, which is the branch of bird photography I find
the most fascinating, and if he is a *Leica* owner, he could hardly
do better than use a Leitz universal focusing bellows in conjunction with the *Visoflex* I reflex housing and either a 135-mm. or
125-mm. *Hektor* lens. A new Leitz lens, the 135-mm. f/4 *Elmar*,
has, however, been produced to replace that old favourite, the
f/4·5 *Hektor* of the same focal length. There is no doubt that in
the new *Elmar* the corrections are considerably improved, contrast is enhanced and residual chromatic errors substantially
eliminated. The lens is designed for both models of the *Visoflex*,
using a short lens mount, or the lens unit alone is available for
the *Visoflex* II with the appropriate extension tube.

The task of the photographer is greatly simplified when using
the Leitz focusing bellows because the left-hand side of the guide-
rail is calibrated in scales of reproduction for the outfit when used
with the 135-mm. *Hektor* or *Elmar*. A white index line above these
calibrations shows the scale of reproduction in decimal figures,
e.g. 0·5 means that the subject is reproduced on the film in half its
natural size. Obviously, for close-ups at long bellows extensions
the exposure time must be increased. These exposure factors are
marked in red on the same scale as the reproduction ratio; for
instance, at a reproduction scale of 0·5 the exposure factor is × 2

69

or slightly over. When making transparencies I always favour slight under-exposure and would not use a higher factor than × 2 at an image ratio of 0·5. Table 10 gives scale of reproduction, distance from subject to film plane and field size for the two *Hektor* lenses, 135 mm. and 125 mm., when used with the *Visoflex* I and focusing bellows. The values, which are approximate, are taken down to a field size of 4·7 × 7·1, which would cover our smallest garden birds. For fields below these dimensions, we are entering the realm of the real close-up, which is outside the scope of this book.

Table 10. Data for 135-mm. and 125-mm. *Hektor* with *Visoflex* I

Setting on scale marked f=135 mm.	135-mm. Hektor without focusing mount		
	Field size (inches)	Subject to film distance (inches)	Image scale
0·05	18·9 × 28·4	117·3	1 : 20
0·1	9·5 × 14·2	64·4	1 : 10
0·2	4·7 × 7·1	38·4	1 : 5
Setting on scale marked f=125 mm.	125-mm. Hektor without focusing mount with adapter ring		
0·05	18·9 × 28·4	104·0	1 : 20
0·1	9·5 × 14·2	57·0	1 : 10
0·2	4·7 × 7·1	33·9	1 : 5

A bellows focusing unit has been produced by Leitz for continuous focusing with the *Visoflex* II and a 90-mm. lens unit over a range from infinity up to same size (1 : 1) reproduction. Two separate adjustments are incorporated: the lens carrier slides on the upper half of the monobar, while on the lower side the tripod attachment has a rack-and-pinion adjustment. The advantage of this is that focusing can be carried out without altering the scale of reproduction. Changing from the vertical to horizontal format

The Equipment

is done by swinging both camera and *Visoflex* as one unit after releasing a catch.

The focusing bellows for the *Visoflex* II carries two sets of scales. On the left-hand side is one which shows the reproduction ratios and corresponding exposure-increase factors for the 90-mm. *Elmarit* or *Elmar* lens heads. On the right-hand side the actual bellows extension is engraved in millimetres, which applies irrespective of the focal length of the lens head used. The bird photographer is more likely to use a 135-mm. lens with these bellows than one of 90-mm. focal length, so the scale on the left does not help him. However, the makers supply tables giving exposure factors at various bellows extensions for lenses other than those of 90 mm., and from this data it is possible to draw up a table of effective lens apertures at various extensions in conjunction with the lens apertures engraved on the lens mount. I have done this on the same lines as those shown in Table 12 for a 105-mm. lens. It would, I think, be helpful if the bellows manufacturers were to supply alternative sets of scales for lens heads of all focal lengths, which could be screwed on to the bellows track, so that the photographer could read all the necessary data for the lens he is using at a glance without having to consult tables.

I would like to make a suggestion to other users of the *Visoflex* II in case they have not thought of it themselves. This reflex mirror attachment carries at the side an arm with a release button, which is fitted with a setting screw. When the *Visoflex* is fitted to the camera this arm is so positioned that the release button is immediately over the camera shutter release, and is so adjusted that pressure on it first flips the reflex mirror out of the way before the camera shutter is operated. To do this it is essential to leave a clearance of about 1 mm. between the bottom of the release arm button and the shutter release. This figure of 1 mm. is quite critical because too great a clearance would involve a time lag between the mirror movement and the shutter operation. Too small a clearance might result in the mirror not having time to get out of the way before the shutter runs down. A conical socket for the cable release in the side of this model of the *Visoflex* controls the entire operation, though it can of course also be done by hand.

71

The Equipment

It is, however, possible to trip the focusing mirror by hand without in any way interfering with the camera shutter. I suggest, therefore, when prefocusing on a perch and before one retreats to a place of concealment, that the mirror be tripped so that it is out of the way. If this is done the cable release can be screwed direct into the camera in the ordinary way. All users of single-lens reflex cameras will know that it is the noise of the mirror tripping which startles the bird more than either the shutter or the flash. Moving the mirror in the way I have suggested precludes any possibility of bird movement between the mirror flipping and the shutter operating, though of course if one forgets to move the mirror after focusing, no picture at all will be obtained.

Table 11 shows the depth of field obtainable at scales of reproduction from 1 : 20 up to one-fifth life size or 1 : 5, the values being based on a circle of confusion of 1/750 in. This table also gives the exposure factors, e.g. for photographing at an image scale of 1/10th life size, we need to multiply the exposure by 1·2. This table, of course, is valid for any lens as we are concerned here only with image ratios.

Table 11. Depths of Field at Various Image Scales

Image scale	Depth of field zone (inches) at					Exposure increase factor
	$f/4$	$f/5·6$	$f/8$	$f/11$	$f/16$	
1 : 20	4·41	6·18	8·85	12·1	17·7	1·1
1 : 17	3·22	4·50	6·43	8·85	12·8	1·1
1 : 15	2·52	3·53	5·05	6·95	10·1	1·1
1 : 12	1·64	2·30	3·28	4·50	6·55	1·2
1 : 10	1·15	1·62	2·32	3·18	4·62	1·2
1 : 8	0·758	1·06	1·51	2·08	3·03	1·3
1 : 6	0·441	0·620	0·885	1·21	1·77	1·4
1 : 5	0·315	0·440	0·632	0·867	1·26	1·4

The Equipment

Focusing bellows are most useful with SLR cameras because no reflex focusing attachment is required, focusing being done on the ground-glass viewfinder in the ordinary way. The bellows replaces the focusing mount of all lenses of long focal length, though one cannot focus on infinity with a lens shorter than 105-mm. focal length with, for example, the *Novoflex* bellows, though short focal-length lenses can be used with focusing mounts to obtain extreme close-ups. Many of my bird photographs have been taken with an *Exakta*, *Novoflex* bellows and 105-mm. f/3·5 *Trinol* lens without focusing mount. The bellows are engraved on one side for the exposure factors for the 105-mm. lens and on the other for 50-mm. lenses. Anyone who uses such a combination as this, i.e. camera, bellows and lens, will soon find it a considerable help to draw up a table which takes exposure factors into account, so that he can see at once what aperture to use in any given light situation. The data I have drawn up for my own use are shown in Table 12.

Table 12. Effective Apertures for 105-mm. *Trinol* Lens

| Bellows extension | Lens opened to | | | | | | |
	f/3·5	f/4	f/5·6	f/8	f/11	f/16	f/22
1·2	4·2	4·8	6·8	9·6	13·2	19·2	26·4
1·4	4·9	5·6	7·8	11·2	15·4	22·4	30·8
1·6	5·6	6·4	9·0	12·8	17·6	25·6	35·2
1·8	6·3	7·2	10·0	14·4	19·8	28·8	39·6
2·0	7·0	8·0	11·2	16·0	22·0	32·0	44·0
2·2	7·7	8·8	12·3	17·6	24·2	35·2	48·4
2·4	8·4	9·6	13·4	19·2	26·4	38·4	52·8
2·6	9·1	10·4	14·6	20·8	28·6	41·6	57·2

Example. If the bellows were extended to the '1·2' mark and the lens aperture stopped down to f/8, the exposure would have to be calculated for f/9·6 or as near that figure as possible. When

73

using *Kodachrome* daylight film with a guide number of 30 for a *Mecablitz* 500 placed 3 ft. from the target, I set the lens aperture at very slightly over f/8 to obtain an effective aperture of f/10 at a bellows extension of 1·2, i.e. very slight underexposure.

'PORTRAIT' LENS OR 'EXTENSIONS'?

Many photographers may wonder why they should go to the trouble and expense of interposing extension tubes or bellows between their cameras and lenses when a 'portrait' lens pushed over the front of the camera's standard lens might do just as well. Supplementary lenses involve no exposure increase whereas, with extension tubes and bellows, the effective aperture of the lens is reduced: sums must be done or tables consulted and the exposure made for an f/ number which will be different from that engraved on the lens mount.

The effect of adding a portrait lens is to shorten the focal length of the combined camera lens and supplementary and, photographically, the result is the equivalent of a short focal-length lens on an extension; one must take the camera closer to the subject and one must be content with a shallower depth of field. Lenses of normal focal lengths which produce sharp images when wide open are most unlikely to achieve such good results when used with a portrait lens and must be stopped down, usually to f/8 or smaller, to register fine detail.

With the camera lens set at infinity and using a 1-dioptre supplementary, the lens must be at a distance of 1 metre from the subject; with a 2-dioptre supplementary, less than 20 in. from the subject, and so on. While the 1- and 2-dioptre supplementaries may be permissible for certain aspects of bird photography, anything stronger is really out of the question, because not only will definition be lost, but the distortion of perspective will be quite appalling. On the other hand, supplementary lenses of low and moderate strengths are perfectly satisfactory with lenses of normal focal length, e.g. 50 mm., provided the lens is stopped down.

The main advantage of the extension between camera and lens is, of course, that one can obtain as large an image as with the supplementary lens but from a greater distance. In the case of a bellows used with a lens of long focal length but without focusing mount, in which form it is much cheaper to buy than with the mount, it is often possible to focus all the way from infinity to an image ratio of 1 : 1. Of course, one must take into consideration the effect of the extension on the lens aperture. Obviously, a 105-mm. f/3·5 lens, for example, when used on a bellows or tube extension, is 'farther away' from the image plane than when it is fitted direct to the camera with its own focusing mount: the f/3·5 no longer holds good, because this figure is calculated for the focal length of 105 mm. which, on an extension, may be increased to 130 mm. or more. Most bellows are engraved with exposure factors, such as × 1·2, × 1·4, × 1·6 and so on, so that if the bellows are extended to × 1·2 mark, it really means that the effective aperture of the wide-open f/3·5 lens becomes f/4·2, i.e. 3·5 × 1·2, and one must calculate the exposure not for the marked aperture, but for the effective aperture. The data is shown in Table 12. As a matter of fact, it is a mistake to think that if one were using an f/3·5 lens wide open at an extension of × 2 one would get the greater depth of field and perhaps better definition of an aperture of f/7. One only uses the higher f/ number when calculating exposure, and an f/3·5 lens should be stopped down to at least f/5·6 to obtain good definition. This would mean, at an extension of × 1·2, an effective aperture of f/6·7 and it is this figure which should be used in connection with exposure times and flash guide numbers.

EFFECTIVE APERTURES

Earlier in this chapter I said that if we increase the distance between the lens and the image plane, i.e. the film, by accessories such as tubes and bellows, the f/ numbers engraved on the lens mount no longer hold good. A diaphragm opening of, say, f/8 is based on the ratio of the lens aperture to the focal length of the lens, i.e. the distance between the lens and film plane when the lens is focused on infinity. If we now move the lens farther away from the film plane by means of rings, tubes or bellows, obviously 'f/8' is incorrect. This figure is in effect a measure of the light transmitted to the film and it will be obvious that if we increase

The Equipment

the distance between the lens and the film the real aperture is no longer f/8 but something smaller. It is quite easy to calculate what the real or effective aperture becomes when using extensions by simple proportion, in this way:

$$\text{Effective aperture} = \frac{\text{marked aperture} \times \text{lens-to-film distance}}{\text{focal length of lens}}$$

If we take as an example a 105-mm. lens extended by tubes or bellows to a distance of 126 mm. from the film plane to focus on a bird about 3 ft. away; and if we get what we consider an adequate depth of field at the mark f/8 on the lens mount, then we must calculate the exposure, not for f/8, but for the relatively smaller aperture, like this:

$$\text{Effective aperture} = \frac{8 \times 126}{105} = 9\cdot6.$$

What we are interested in, then, is what the light meter says we should use at f/9·6 and not f/8. It would be safe to use f/10, I think, because I prefer when using colour reversal film to underexpose slightly.

Another way to work out the exposure required at the smaller effective aperture is by the following formula:

$$\text{Exposure increase factor} = \frac{(\text{lens-to-film distance})^2}{(\text{focal length of lens})^2}$$

The result of this equation would give us the figure by which the exposure should be multiplied so that the required amount of light can reach the film at the effective aperture. Assume the solution to this equation to be 2. If therefore the exposure required at the engraved aperture were 1/50, then the real exposure needed would be $2 \times 1/50 = 1/25$ sec.

VIBRATION

Except when the camera is being held in the hand for photographing birds in flight, a tripod must always be used. The need for securing extreme sharpness in the transparency or negative has already been mentioned and it is quite impossible to achieve this unless the camera is rock steady when the exposure is made. Despite their claims, very few photographers can avoid some

2. Arrangement of camera and flash for photographing birds through a window as described on p. 89. The cloth hide, connection from camera to flash and the shutter release have been omitted to avoid complicating the illustration. The auxiliary flash head, when used with this set-up, is placed outdoors. The colour pictures of the chaffinch, nuthatch and great tit were taken with this equipment.

The Equipment

camera shake when they release the shutter and in some cameras the focal plane shutter itself can set up vibration. The effect of camera movement at the moment of exposure varies with the focal length of the lens: it is least evident with a wide-angle lens, but with a lens of long focal length or a telescopic lens the slightest shake at the camera becomes greatly magnified at the front of the lens, which may be some inches from the film plane. As a general rule any movement of the camera causing a shift of the image on the film of up to half the diameter of the circle of confusion will not be noticed. If we focus a 35-mm. camera with a 50-mm. lens at its nearest focusing distance, somewhere about one metre, the image ratio is 1 : 20. If we now, by the use of accessories, obtain an image twice the size, i.e. 1 : 10, then not only the image, but everything else is doubled, including the result of movement, either by the camera or the subject. The closer the camera is taken to the subject and the greater the image ratio obtained, the more evident will be movement due to vibration or unsteadiness, until at really large scales of reproduction, the slightest motion, undetected by the eye, will cancel all the trouble taken with focusing and exposure calculation.

For outdoor work where the camera only is hidden behind a hide and operated from a distance by a long shutter release, I use a wooden ex-Army tripod which weighs about 7 lb. It is fitted with a simple ball-and-socket head and is really a most solid affair, its single disadvantage being that when the legs are fully retracted it is still too high for some situations. This wooden tripod has no adjustable centre column so its height must be fixed by shortening or lengthening the legs. This is only possible where the hide is single-sided and in the open: inside an enclosed hide it would drive one frantic, so, for work where I am concealed in the hide together with the camera I use a metal tripod with legs of horse-shoe-shaped section, which retract to about 2 ft. This tripod has an adjustable centre post which, with the pan-and-tilt head, gives any camera height and angle desired.

When photographing through a window I use either a Leitz table tripod with a ball-and-socket head or a heavy circular brass plate about 5 in. diameter with a short projection in the centre threaded to fit the tripod bush of the bellows or camera. The real function of this device is to hold cameras for display purposes on a dealer's shelves but it has proved an ideal camera support for narrow window-sills. I sometimes use the Leitz table tripod from a hide standing on a special home-made base. This base consists of a short heavy plank of wood covered on one side with ½-in. mesh wire netting. The object of the netting is to ensure that once the position of the tripod has been found the feet will not slip. The tripod is of course too short to stand direct on the ground and must be placed on some kind of support.

LENS HOODS

A lens hood will help in securing crisp colour transparencies and negatives because by cutting off unwanted light rays and preventing them from entering the lens, either directly or by reflection, contrast is increased and this is an important quality in registering fine detail. Most lens hoods are simple cone-shaped affairs which push on to or screw into the front of the lens mount. These are quite satisfactory provided they are dead black inside and will not reflect light striking their inner surfaces. Most of the more expensive lens hoods have internal corrugations to break up extraneous light rays. The ideal lens hood would have a rectangular hole of the same proportions as the film instead of a circular opening to admit the light: that is to say, a hood for a 35-mm. camera might have an opening of 50×72 mm. All other things being equal, the longer the lens hood the better, but it must allow the entire 24×36-mm. film to be covered and not cut off any light at the corners. If focusing bellows are used, a bellows-type lens hood can be slid on the guide rails in front of the lens panel and should be extended as far as possible, taking care that no vignetting occurs. On my longest lens I often use a home-made hood made from a thin aluminium can about $2\frac{1}{2}$ in. diam. $\times$ 3 in. long, lined with black velvet. This fits over the lens and is held in position by a small grub screw. A rectangular opening has been cut in the centre of the other end of the can. If one does use a home-made hood it is essential that it be very light in weight because there is the risk of distorting the camera front if it has to support too much in the shape of long lenses combined with long hoods.

The Equipment

For 'posed' portraits of birds, that is to say, when the camera is mounted on a tripod or other support, firing the shutter by pressing the release button is almost certain to lead to camera shake and only in emergencies should this method be used. The cable or flexible wire type release should be an essential part of the equipment and it must never be shorter than 8 in.; 12 in. is better still and I always use an 18-in. cable when working from a hide. A too-short release may transmit movement to the camera, and whatever the length of the cable it should never be stretched tight in case it leads to jerking the camera with perhaps disastrous results.

When the camera only is hidden and I am working from a distance, I use a pneumatic type of release, which consists of the familiar rubber bulb at the operator's end and a plunger actuating the shutter at the other. The tube connecting the two is in two sections which can be joined to give a total length of about 33 ft. I invariably use this release when photographing through a window or when the camera is set up near the house. It has always been satisfactory, but it is advisable to test it before connection to the camera to make sure that when the bulb is squeezed at one end the plunger will do its work at the other.

Some photographers prefer the electrical type of shutter release when working at distances of over about 15 ft., but these are elaborate and expensive. Other types of electrical release automatically fire the shutter when the bird settles on a spot upon which the camera has been focused, or when it flies through an invisible beam. These are in the luxury class and few amateurs can afford them.

Methods for releasing the shutter from a distance necessitate visiting the camera to wind on the film and to reset the shutter. This is often a disadvantage because if the bird has not been disturbed by the shutter noise and, when used, the flash, it will sometimes take up a better position for portraiture and one could make another shot of it. But one has to take a chance on this, though it is a mistake to emerge from a hiding-place too soon if the bird doesn't fly away, because he may, as I have said elsewhere,

The Equipment

associate shutter noise and flash with the approach of a human. It is better to be patient: let him finish what he is doing and only emerge from the hide when he has flown away.

There are devices for carrying out all operations from a distance, including winding on the film and resetting the shutter. A clockwork mechanism at the camera fires the shutter then resets it, winding on the film in the ordinary way at the same time. These operations are set in motion by the operator pressing a button, the signal being transmitted electrically to the clockwork, and an entire film of 20 exposures can be dealt with by a single winding of the 'clock'.

If any of these remote controls are used it is necessary to use electronic flash because if the photographer has to visit the 'works' to change the flashbulb, obviously the whole purpose of remote control is wasted.

CHAPTER 4

Hides

To be able to approach a bird to take its portrait, some kind of hide is necessary, whether the quarry is sitting on a nest or attracted to a specially-arranged bait, upon which the camera may have been pre-focused. Hides vary according to the requirements of the job in hand and to the photographer's taste but, whichever such devices are used, it is essential that they provide proper concealment for both the photographer and his equipment in all conditions of weather and in a reasonable degree of comfort. Hides for garden photography are in general of three main kinds. First, there is the permanent sort, such, for instance, as a shed or other small structure built near a spot frequented by birds —a pond, for example, where they come to bathe. Second, there is the portable kind for erection at different spots in the garden according to requirements, and which will house not only the camera and flash equipment, when it is used, but also the photographer himself. Third, is the simple one-sided affair usually consisting of two poles and a single sheet of cloth behind which the camera is placed, the photographer operating the apparatus from a distance through some kind of long shutter release. This also, of course, may be moved about the garden.

PERMANENT STRUCTURES

If photography is done from a permanent structure, the birds must be attracted to a nearby spot to be photographed. A garden toolshed will do admirably for this kind of hide and within easy camera range of it should be some feature to entice the birds. A nesting box on a nearby tree or fence is excellent; or a small bird

F   81

table, but these two should not be close together or the box will not be used. No bird will build her nest near any feature of the garden which is much frequented by other birds. It should be possible to fix a box within reasonable camera range of the shed on one side and a small bird table, also within range, on the other. This will mean, of course, having two sets of apertures in the walls of the shed to accommodate the camera, flash and also perhaps for observation purposes. I have fixed a nest box within a few feet of the door of my toolshed, while a little farther away and in a slightly different direction is a pond which is screened from the nest box by the trunks of a pair of silver birches. Both spots, however, are commanded by a single set of holes in the toolshed door by swinging the camera tripod top through about 60 degrees. A 105-mm. lens is of long enough focal length for the box, which is generally used by great tits; and a 135-mm. lens gives me a large enough image of the birds bathing, which they always do at the end of the pond nearest the toolshed. It usually happens that several birds are bathing together in a group which fills the 35-mm. frame. The aperture for the camera lens is oblong so that the camera has a clear view of either box or pond. A similar hole is provided for the electronic flashgun, and a peephole above the camera aperture for observation purposes. Each hole has slots on the inner side of the door to carry small sheets of *Perspex* so that the holes can be covered when no photography is being done. When the auxiliary flash head is used it is partially concealed among some conveniently placed shrubs. The layout is shown in Fig. 5.

An advantage of this type of hide, if it can be so called, is that the shed door can be locked and the camera and flash set-up left overnight. Two large polythene bags are used to protect the equipment and, as the door opens outwards, there is no need to disturb anything. During damp weather, of course, the equipment is dismantled and brought indoors but, in dry weather, a great deal of setting-up time is saved by leaving the apparatus *in situ*.

Growing shrubs will sometimes serve as a hide for the camera though they are seldom thick enough or of such a shape as to conceal the photographer in comfort. I have used a rhododendron as a camera hide for photographing birds feeding on a wire basket

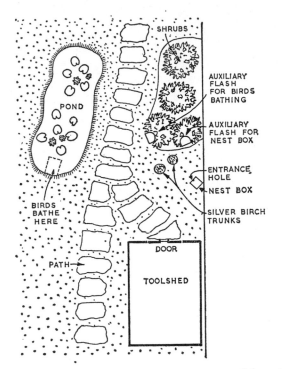

FIG. 5a. Sketch to show how two targets are covered from the same hide with lenses of different focal lengths. The arrangement of the birds' bathing pool is shown in greater detail in Fig. 1.

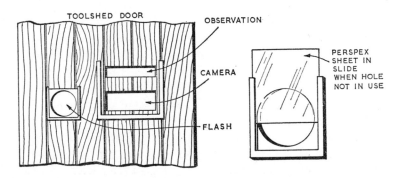

FIG. 5b. Part of the toolshed door showing the apertures for camera, flash and observation when photographing the sites in Fig. 5a.

containing scraps, the bright parts of the camera being covered with a piece of green casement: some of the smaller rhododendron branches are tied together to give thicker cover where needed. In this case the shutter is operated by a long pneumatic release from a place of concealment. Semi-permanent hides can be contrived of brushwood or similar material where there is enough available, but as a rule an artificial hide of the type described in the next paragraph is quicker to erect and causes less disturbance to the birds.

ENCLOSED MOVABLE HIDES

My second hide is a movable one and large enough to accommodate both me and the camera outfit. Any hide of this type, in addition to providing protection from the weather, must also conceal the photographer and his equipment in all kinds of light. By that I mean that if the hide lies between a low sun and the nest, no silhouette of the man within must be apparent to the bird. Secondly, no part of the hide must flap in the wind; the sides must be stretched tightly between the supports and the bottom of the hide must, if necessary, be pegged to the ground. Thirdly, the material from which the hide is made should provide some degree of shelter, especially to the equipment, in the event of a shower. Such a specification requires a structure which is completely enclosed when in use. My hide, which is based on the types used by photographers of wild birds, is however somewhat simpler in design but quite effective. It is illustrated in Fig. 6.

The main supports are four lengths of $\frac{1}{2}$-in. bore water pipe 5 ft. long. The tops of these are connected when the hide is erected by four pieces of hardwood, two 3 ft. long and two 3 ft. 6 in. long. Each length of wood has a $\frac{1}{4}$-in.-diameter hole bored through it about 1 in. from each end. Four 6-in. round nails complete the structural members. When the uprights are driven into the ground the lengths of wood are used as gauges, so that the dimensions of the hide are just under 3 ft. by a little less than 3 ft. 6 in. The tops of the pipe uprights are then held by the wooden pieces, the nails being dropped through the holes to make the structure firm. Over this is then placed the fabric cover.

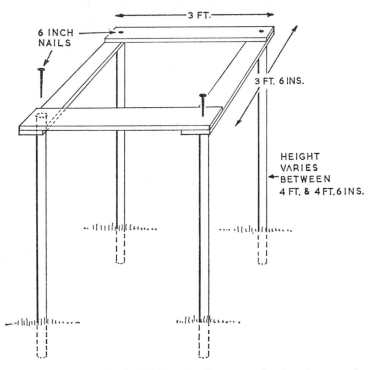

FIG. 6. Framework of the hide affording cover for the photographer and his equipment for photographing birds in the open.

FABRIC COVERS

This cover is assembled from two pieces of dark green casement cloth. One piece is 13 ft. long × 3 ft 6 in. wide to make two 5 × 3 ft. 6 in. sides and a 3 × 3 ft 6 in. top. The other piece is 13 ft 6 in. long × 3 ft wide to make the two 5 × 3 ft. ends and a 3 × 3ft. 6 in. top. A slight margin all round is allowed for machining to make a workmanlike job. When these two pieces are sewn together they form a kind of box 5 ft. deep, 3 ft. wide and 3 ft. 6 in. long. The top of this box will be of double thickness and the bottom will be open. Only three of the vertical seams are sewn, the fourth being left open to afford ingress and egress. The top of the hide, being of double thickness casement, would give cover against a light shower, but heavy or prolonged rain would collect, cause the material to sag in the centre, and eventually water would drip through. To prevent this, a 3 × 3 ft. 6 in. piece of waterproof material is stuck to the top of the hide with *Bostik*. It will be obvious that, the cloth cover being of the same length as the uprights, it will be too deep when pulled down tightly over the frame and will leave some 6 in. or more of material lying loose on the ground. To prevent this from flapping in the wind, it is drawn tightly round the posts from inside the hide and pinned to the ground with a metal skewer at each corner. After entering the hide, the open corner is closed with safety pins.

HIDE ACCESSORIES

Its use being confined to the garden, this hide answers perfectly well. There is no stony ground into which the uprights must be driven and no guy ropes are ever necessary. A hide of smaller dimensions would do for a younger and more supple occupant than I am but, if it is to be occupied for any length of time it must be as comfortable as possible. Many photographers use a folding stool, but I manage with a stout wooden box and a *Dunlopillo* cushion. When the hide is dismantled, the cover is folded and kept in this box, together with the 6-in. nails and skewers and any oddments I have from time to time found necessary.

On the front of the hide are two slits each about 9 in. long, one each for the camera and the flashlamp, enabling me to cover a large enough area with both. The hide is used mostly for watching one specific spot, such as a nest or a perch, either a natural or an artificial one, so that the camera can be prefocused and the flash, when used, already aimed at the target. Those parts of the slits in the cloth not in use are closed with safety pins. An observation hole is not always needed because I can watch for the quarry in the ground-glass finder of the reflex I generally use for this kind of work.

The photographer must decide for himself whether or not he wishes to have observation holes in addition to the slits made for the camera and flash. It is, of course, an advantage to have some kind of peephole on each side of the hide so that a watch can be kept for the bird's approach to the nest. Too many holes will naturally detract from the purpose of the hide, but square or oblong holes can be cut and framed by a slot on three sides to hold a piece of tinted plastic for use as a window. In this way a lookout can be kept and a forewarning received that extra care must be taken not to increase the bird's suspicions by making any undue noise. When the bird is on or near the nest it can, of course, be seen from the front of the hide, either in the ground-glass viewfinder if a reflex camera is in use or by gently making a small opening in the pinned-up fabric enclosing the camera lens.

From a hide of the type described it is possible to command a view of both nest and a nearby perch if this is desired, by enlarging the opening for the lens in such a way that the tripod top can be swung in a small arc. The best way of doing this quietly and with the minimum of disturbance is to have this opening in the form of an elongated rectangle and to conceal all the camera parts except the lens with a piece of thin material of the same colour as the hide which is secured round the four sides of the rectangle. This material should be loose with a hole made for the lens to which it is held by a strong rubber band, in the same way as the openings in a changing bag can be secured to the wrists.

HIDE FOR CAMERA ONLY

My second portable hide is a much simpler affair and consists of two uprights and a single piece of casement cloth. It is, in fact, a shield and is used to conceal the camera and flash, the shutter being operated from a distance by a long pneumatic release. I use two of the uprights from the 'four-poster' hide described, one of the lengths of hardwood and two of the 6-in. nails. This hide, in fact, resembles one side of the box-type hide, but there are one or two important differences. Small curtain rings are sewn along the edge of the cloth and these are slipped over the uprights after they have been driven into the ground. The cloth is also longer than the height of the uprights by some 3 ft. This is brought up and over the outside of the horizontal wooden tie and covers the

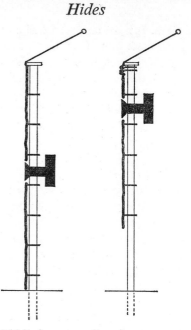

FIG. 7. Sketch of hide for concealing the camera only, the shutter being operated by a long release from a place of cover. The front of the hide is adjustable for low and high positions of the camera.

camera and flash equipment, and the ends are secured by attaching loops at the end of the cloth to some part of the tripod with rubber bands, so that one corner can be lifted easily for winding on the shutter and checking the focus.

The hole for the camera lens is different in this hide. Instead of a slit in the cloth to allow for varying heights of the camera and flash, both holes are in fixed positions and different levels are obtained by raising or lowering the fabric as shown in the sketch (Fig. 7). The peephole for the lens is made by cutting two slits in the cloth at right-angles to each other. The opening is made too small to allow the widest part of the lens hood to pass through, so this is placed on the lens from the front of the hide after the camera is in position so that there are no loose pieces of cloth to flap in front of the lens. The same type of hole is used for the flash head. As the angular relationship of the camera and the main

Hides

flash head is the same for all pictures taken with this hide, whether or not the auxiliary flash head is used, there is no need to make more than two holes in the screen fabric. When the camera is in the highest position the screen is clear of the ground, as shown. In this case the tripod legs can be seen from the front but, as these are of wood painted a dark olive green, no bright metal parts are visible.

Whenever possible, I use an auxiliary flash head to give side lighting to the subject. This is usually hung from the branch of a shrub or the top of a bamboo stake. It should be made quite secure and prevented from swinging from side to side in the wind. If not, the flash may be pointing in quite the wrong direction just when it is needed.

I've never done any photography of nests in trees which required a pylon-type hide or involved building platforms in trees. My nearest venture to this type of photography was making a picture of an open-fronted nest box on the house wall which a pair of flycatchers had used. The single nestling was making ready to leave and, to take his picture, I used a folding aluminium ladder, the camera being clamped to one of the rungs by an ancient device intended for attaching a camera to a car windscreen pillar.

Window Hide

My hide for photographing from inside a window is the simplest of all and consists of a sheet of black cloth fixed across the window-frame with drawing pins. A hole of the same design as in the hide just described accommodates the lens, and enough of the window is covered to allow me to approach the camera for winding on the shutter and focusing without being seen from outside. The flash set is mounted on a tripod separately and, as it is farther from the bait than the camera, no attempt is made to conceal it. It will be realized that the window glass in front of both the lens and the flash must be spotless and free from flaws.

I might mention here that no extra lens filter is required for taking colour photographs through ordinary window glass.

CHAPTER 5

Lighting

When taking colour pictures outdoors the greatest and the most uncontrollable variable is the daylight. When static subjects are being dealt with, i.e. those which will stay put until the sun comes out again or until a new light-meter reading is taken, the problem is not serious; but when birds are the subjects, likely to fly away at the slightest disturbance, the photographer really is in difficulties. Daylight is extremely erratic, changing almost from minute to minute, so that a light-meter reading taken from a subject of equivalent hue and brightness of the bird may, by the time the photographer is back in the hide, be quite valueless. An overall light reading taken from an aperture in the hide is very seldom the answer because the bird will be only one of many factors influencing the reading from such a position.

BIRDS ON PERCHES

The problems posed by a bird on a pre-arranged perch, which may be in full sun, are quite different from those of a bird at the nest, which is more likely than not to be in shade, wholly if not partially. When a bird is on a perch in a sunny position he is, when the sun is fully upon him, lit not only by the sun itself, but by light reflected from clouds and perhaps also by nearby objects. If the perch is in full sun in a cloudless sky and there are no reflecting surfaces near by, the shadowed part of the bird, such as his underparts if the sun is overhead, may present too great a contrast for satisfactory overall rendering on colour film. If this is the case, it may be possible to throw back some light from a light-coloured reflector, which should not be too near the perch

90

and should be positioned after tests on some object of roughly the same shape as the bird. If, on the other hand, the sun is behind very light clouds, lighting becomes more uniform and there may be just enough contrast between the upper and lower parts of the bird to give a well-rounded overall picture.

BIRDS ON THEIR NESTS

It is with birds at or on the nest that the greatest lighting difficulties will be found. Even though the required amount of gardening has been done to enable the camera to get a clear view of the nest, it will probably still be in the general shade of trees or bushes. If the sky is cloudless the shadows will register on the colour film as blue. If a reflector is set up to throw light back into the nest there will still in all probability be a bluish tinge, because the film will see the result as a mixture of blue from the sky and colour from the reflector which, if white, will dilute blue until it may no longer be objectionable. This state of affairs can largely be remedied, however, by using a haze or ultra-violet filter over the lens. With colour in the camera I always have this filter in place, not only because it reduces the blue but also because it protects the lens: filters are cheaper than lenses and no extra exposure time has to be allowed for this particular filter.

When photographing in daylight the light falling on the target must be carefully studied, and this with one other important factor—the best view of the nest or individual bird—must be reconciled to make satisfactory exposures possible. Of course, garden birds do not as a rule build in such positions that strong sunlight falls on the nest, which would make the photographer's work too easy. This being the case, the nest should be watched for a day at least and if possible meter readings taken to find out when the nest receives the strongest daylight. If this is combined with a little judicious, i.e. not too obvious, gardening, the best possible conditions will be obtained.

Most garden bird subjects are small and quick-moving. This means that to photograph them unless they are seen on the nest, especially in colour and in close-up, one must use a very short exposure. If the colour film is one of slow speed such as daylight

Lighting

Kodachrome I, which has a *Weston* or ASA rating of 10, a short exposure means a large aperture; and a large aperture in turn may not give us the depth of field we would like. One would seldom use a speed slower than 1/50 sec. unless the bird were on the nest, when we can perhaps risk 1/10 sec. Assuming a lens of maximum aperture or speed of f/3·5, we are likely to get the best all-round results so far as depth of field is concerned at an aperture between the next two smaller stops, at say f/5·6, when the lens is focused on a bird incubating and the field includes part of the surroundings of the nest. Assuming, then, a speed of 1/10 sec. at f/5·6 with daylight *Kodachrome* I in the camera, the light meter, if we are using a *Weston* IV, should give a value of not under 25. If the nest is badly lit, as it normally would be, the light reading might well be under this figure, which means either a larger lens aperture or a slower speed.

PICTURES BY FLASH

The answer to this dilemma is flash, because if he has flash equipment the photographer can ignore the daylight and pictures can be taken at any time of the day or night. Assuming the same conditions as in the last paragraph and a flash guide number for *Kodachrome* I of 30–35, which I have found about right for a 120-joule equipment outdoors, we can set the speed of the focal plane shutter at 1/50 sec. and, with the flash head 5 ft. from the nest, close the lens aperture down to f/6·3. We have then in these circumstances a smaller lens opening to give the depth of field we require, a light source of constant value, while the effective shutter speed will be actually the duration of the flash, i.e. about 1/750 sec., which is fast enough to arrest any movement of a sitting bird. With the new *Kodachrome* II I find a guide number of 50–60 gives good results outdoors or through a window.

The choice between flashbulbs and electronic flash is largely a matter of individual experience. The original cost of a flashbulb set is very much lower than that of an electronic set, though the latter is cheaper to operate in the long run. The electronic flash set is heavier as well as being more costly, but both weight and price have been reduced in the latest sets.

Lighting

Many photographers place their flash heads on top of or alongside their cameras, but better overall lighting is achieved when the flash head is about 2 ft. to the right or left of the camera. Such an arrangement also avoids the danger of 'red eye' with which portrait photographers are familiar. A second or auxiliary flash head will give depth to the subject if carefully placed. When taking flash pictures of birds, I set up the main flash head about 2 ft. to the right or left of the camera and at the same level, and the auxiliary flash head a little farther away from the subject and at an angle of about 90 degrees to the camera-subject axis. The electronic set I use has a speed of 1/750 sec. at which speed daylight has little opportunity to register on *Kodachrome*: more often than not the background to the bird is black, even though the picture be taken in broad daylight. If the bird has a black back, such as the great spotted woodpecker for example, his back may be indistinguishable from the background. But the auxiliary flash head, set up near his favourite tree so that it is directed at his back when he is in his usual position, outlines him and also throws a little extra light on the bright red spot on the back of his head.

Guide Numbers

Users of electronic flash should use the published guide numbers for colour film with caution. If one questions these guide numbers with the makers or retailers of these flash sets, having experienced some quite severe examples of under-exposure, one is told that the figures are for 'average' conditions, whatever that may mean. One might just as well talk about an 'average' English summer! The quoted guide numbers, usually in advertisements for an electronic set, are almost invariably optimistic. For example, the rating of my set is 120 joules, and the published guide number for *Kodachrome* I is 46–56. When I was younger and greener and believed the advertisements, I wasted a lot of money on under-exposed transparencies. Of course, guide numbers for the same flash set and film vary very widely and one must experiment: I suggest starting off by halving the advertised guide number unless one is taking pictures in a small white-tiled room. When used outdoors, as in bird photography, there are no reflecting surfaces as a rule,

Lighting

and a very much lower than claimed guide number should be tried. I regularly use a guide number of 30 for *Kodachrome* I and 50–60 for *Kodachrome* II with my set, and I have found this to be just right, with or without the auxiliary flash head.

FLASH FACTORS FOR CLOSE-UPS

There is another point to bear in mind when taking bird portraits. The flash factor or guide number found by experiment may work very well at distances over about 5 ft., but it may break down at shorter distances, say when taking a close-up at such a range that a small bird almost fills the frame. Whether the law is valid at very short distances depends upon the type of reflector used. If the flash reflector is of the type which projects strongly directional illumination in a bundled beam, there may be considerable deviation from the established guide number with resultant under-exposure. In these circumstances, instead of using the orthodox formula of $S = \dfrac{F}{D}$, where S is the lens stop, F the guide number or flash factor and D the distance between lamp and subject, one may be more successful with the formula $S = \dfrac{F}{D(n+1)}$, where n is the ratio of lens stop reduction which, when bellows are used, can be read off from the scale engraved on the side of the extension bar. If one is using tubes, the value of n can be found from the formula: $n+1 = \dfrac{f+d}{f}$, where d is the total extension, engraved on the tubes, and f is the focal length of the lens. If the flash reflector is of the type where the light is evenly and strongly scattered over the solid angle of throw, the ordinary inverse square law is valid even with close-ups and when the lamp is within 1 ft. of the subject.

Two important points must be borne in mind with flash illumination. First, the subject distance is measured from the flash and not from the camera, and the measurement is taken from the apex at the back of the flash head. For doing this one of those flexible steel rules which stays put when extended is invaluable.

Lighting

Secondly, it must not be forgotten in connection with guide numbers that the effective aperture and not the engraved aperture of the lens must figure in the calculations. Unless the flash is mounted on the camera, some may find difficulty in deciding just where to place the lamp or lamps. The easiest way of doing this is to use a hand torch, studying the lighting given from various angles and then positioning the flash accordingly.

FLASH FOR FILL-IN LIGHTING

Apart from bird portraiture with flash as the sole illumination, ignoring entirely whatever daylight there is, one can use flash for fill-in to lighten the shadows. The orthodox way of calculating how far from the subject the fill-in flash should be is to take a meter reading of the highlights for the ordinary daylight exposure. If this works out at, say, 1/50 sec. at f/8 and the guide number is, say, 100, then the distance at which the flash should be set from the subject would be found by dividing 100 by 8, or 12½ ft. This would give an equal balance of sunlight and flash or a ratio of 1 : 1. It might, however, in some cases be advisable to use a lower ratio so as to preserve some shadow, especially if the flash were to be placed at 90 degrees to the camera-subject axis. In such an example, a ratio of 2 : 1 would be better, and this is obtained by dividing the guide number by the next larger stop, i.e. f/5·6. This would give a flash distance of about 18 ft.

It is naturally just as necessary for the flash as well as the lens to be able to 'see' the bird and a little extra gardening may be necessary if fill-in flash is used in the way suggested in the preceding paragraph. If the flash cannot be placed far away from the nest or perch because too many obstacles would have to be removed so as to avoid throwing shadows on the subject, it can be set at about half the distance (i.e. at about 9 ft.) if a white handkerchief is fixed over the flash head. In all cases, however, particularly where nests are concerned, the very minimum of interference with the bird should be tolerated, gardening must never be excessive and it is always more considerate to tie twigs or branches out of the way for the time being, restoring them afterwards, than to cut them off.

Lighting

I invariably use an ultraviolet filter over the lens with or without flash when I am taking colour pictures, either in the open or through a window. As I have said on p. 89 no other filter is needed with daylight colour film.

CARE OF FLASH EQUIPMENT

The two worst enemies of flash equipment are rough handling and moisture, so any leads taken from an indoor electric connection to a flash set being operated outdoors must be of waterproof cable. The ordinary household flex will not do. The lead from the flash set to an auxiliary head is always supplied in waterproof cable and if it becomes necessary at any time to renew it the same type of wiring must be used. If any of these leads or any other part of the equipment become damp they must be dried immediately after use.

All flash leads and the connection between the flash and the camera should be as straight as possible and never allowed to become kinked. It is also most important that no kinks form in the long shutter release operated by bulb. This should be carefully straightened when unwound from its drum and tested. When operations are finished this release must be carefully rewound on its drum and not just rolled up and stuffed into a box. Upon this thin tube depends the working of the entire outfit. If for any reason it should fail to work properly the picture will not be taken.

CHAPTER 6

Taking the Picture

I do very little photography of incubating or brooding birds; and resort to this method only when I want to show the bird and its nest in their natural surroundings, to photograph parents feeding young or when the bird cannot be induced to visit one of the feeeding places. I use 35-mm. colour film for all my bird photography as my aim is to picture the subject in its natural colours. With 35-mm. film one must secure as large an image of the bird as possible: in other words, fill in the 1 × 1½-in. frame with the bird alone or with the bird and other objects which contribute to the picture. This, undoubtedly, is best done by inducing the bird to take up such a position that he presents the desired aspect to the camera. If one can afford equipment and colour material in sizes larger than 35 mm. this matter of filling the frame is not so important because the image of the bird itself can be as large as that secured on 35-mm. size together with some surrounding detail which the 35-mm. user must omit. But not many of us can afford colour material in the larger sizes and, even if cash is not a seriously limiting factor, one does not feel unduly extravagant if one takes a few extra shots with 35-mm. film when the subject justifies it in the hope of securing one outstanding picture.

FINDING NESTS

To take pictures of birds during the breeding season one must first locate the nest. The procedure for finding nests in the garden is quite different from and much less laborious than that necessary in open country. For one thing, the area to be searched is confined and one can do it without interruptions or 'assistance'. It is easiest of course, in the case of nesting boxes, because however secretive the birds may be, there is generally some tell-tale evidence of the box being in use. The entrance hole will be comparatively clean and not obstructed by spider webs, and there may even be small pieces of nesting material hanging from the entrance or dropped on the ground underneath. If one is in doubt, some minutes' watching from a place of concealment will usually decide the matter. When searching for nests in hedges one should not pull the branches and twigs about, because this may damage the nests or eggs and might even scare the birds away altogether. Few hedges are so dense that no light penetrates and if one walks slowly along on the shady side the outline of a nest will generally be quite easily spotted silhouetted against the light.

Many birds themselves provide clues to where they are building. They can be seen collecting nesting materials and careful observation will show where they are taking it. Once the search has been narrowed to a small area, it should be easy enough to find the nest.

Nests in Holes

Next after the birds who nest in boxes the easiest nests to find should be those built in holes in banks and trees, but such sites are probably only available in the larger gardens. If the photographer is fortunate enough to have a stream passing through his grounds with earth banks, he may find kingfishers building in a hole. If so, he is to be congratulated because there is no more colourful bird in the British Isles and one particularly suitable for colour photography. I have had kingfishers in my garden because a canal flows along the end of it, but they only come to sit in a tree overlooking my pond to inspect the fish. Another bird with brilliant plumage to make his nest in holes, but this time in trees, is the great spotted woodpecker. None of my trees, I'm sorry to say, provides a suitable nesting site, though both the green and great spotted woodpeckers come to feed in my garden, and I have made several good pictures of the latter bird. Two other birds that build in holes or crevices are the nuthatch and tree-creeper. The nuthatch has been known to use a box, but I have had no such luck, possibly because the garden is so full of great tits and blue tits. The tree-creeper will build in a crevice behind bark and, though I have provided several of what I considered suitable sites, none of these birds has nested in my garden. It is obvious, though, that those birds who build in holes are among our most attractive species, especially the kingfisher, woodpeckers and nuthatch.

NESTS IN BUSHES AND UNDERGROWTH

At one time I used to prune my climbing and hedge roses in the spring, but in doing so I often came across a half-built nest, occasionally damaging it or at the least exposing it to such an extent that it was abandoned: I gave up the practice because of this and now do all my rose-pruning in the autumn as soon as the leaves have fallen. This method has more than one advantage: first, it is done when other work is not so pressing as it is in April and I am convinced that the roses are stronger and healthier; and secondly, the birds can now build undisturbed.

Not all birds choose trees, hedges or shrubs for nesting. Some build on the ground and I have found nests of both robin and willow warbler in the rough heather and long grass under birches in my garden. These nests are the most difficult of all to find because the owners generally alight on the ground away from the nest and make their way to it secretly. Sometimes, after careful watching a clue is given by, say, a continually alighting in a certain area, but more often such nests are found accidentally or after a search, covering all likely areas slowly and with great care.

PLACING THE HIDE

In photographing a nest, it is not always possible to place the hide in its final position at once, and several moves may be necessary to allay the bird's suspicions and to prevent the nest from being abandoned. We are dealing only with garden birds which are generally more approachable than the truly wild ones, but all birds will be naturally suspicious of a strange erection within a few feet of their nests, and it is wiser to reach the desired position in two or more moves, depending upon the location. If there is already a certain amount of natural screen for the nest, as there is where birds have built in undergrowth or low shrubs, the final approach is easier. But if the nest is higher up commanding a wider view of its surroundings three moves may be necessary.

In any case it is seldom wise to complete the hide at once. If the skeleton structure is erected one day without undue nervousness being shown by the sitting bird, then the cover may be put on next day. During all this time the photographer should keep himself informed of the state of progress so as to select the best time for moving the hide to its final position. He will, of course, know the bird he is stalking; and he should also find out the normal incubation period, because just before the eggs are hatched is the time when the bird is most intent on her job and the more reluctant to desert the potential family over which she has already spent so much time. Moreover it is usually the case that the best time for moving the hide or undertaking any constructional work is the evening, when it is just light enough to work. The work must be done quietly and never hurried.

FINAL POSITION OF HIDE

The final distance between the hide and the nest or other site depends upon what kind of a picture is needed. For birds at or on the nest the picture should include not only the nest but a substantial part of the surroundings, enough at least for anyone to see what species of shrub contains the nest or the nature of the immediate surroundings if the nest is among long grass or other undergrowth. If it is desired to photograph the bird on a natural or a contrived perch near the nest, much the same rule applies. Most attractive pictures can be made of one of the parents approaching the nest with food and it will generally be found that the bird in doing this will first alight on a convenient branch or other perch before the final flight to the nest. If a natural perch is not available it is easy to provide one by sticking a piece of branch into the ground. In this case the picture area should also be large enough to give an indication of the surrounding terrain. Needless to say the artificial perch should be of the same kind of tree or shrub as the surrounding growth.

100

Taking the Picture

The only satisfactory way of determining how near the hide must be is to use the camera as a guide, and to watch the picture in the viewfinder until the best aspect is found, considering both the nature of the light and the size of the main object in relation to the entire picture area. When this position is found it should be marked by pushing a stick or some other easily recognized object into the ground. When the hide is erected in its final position the hole or slit for the camera should coincide with this marker.

If one is to use flash, the position of this too must be borne in mind. There must be no obstruction of any kind between the flash head and the nest or other target, otherwise no light at all may reach the bird or at best an ugly shadow will be cast. Consequently, a line of view from the known position of the flash head with the camera on the marker must be taken and, if there is any obstruction, it must either be removed or the position altered until both camera and flash have a clear view. It goes without saying that the picture must be studied with the lens it is intended to use in position on the camera. It would be useless to fix the site for the camera with, say, a 90-mm. lens and then decide to change to one of 135 mm. after the marker has been placed.

In conducting all these operations the garden bird photographer is much more fortunate than his colleague hunting wild birds. He is not exposed to inquisitive passers-by, who may offer suggestions, or to the curiosity of horses or cows which can never resist investigating some strange phenomenon. The garden bird photographer can almost always work in peace, giving all his concentration to the job in hand.

'GARDENING'

In nearly all cases some so-called 'gardening' will be necessary to present a good view to the camera. There will always be a few twigs obstructing a good view of the nest and these may be removed when the bird is not sitting. When I do this I cut the twig with a small pair of sharp secateurs and tuck the cut piece into the rest of the bush so that its removal may not be too obvious or the bird may sense that a potential enemy is lurking and depart. Again, leafy twigs or branches which serve some practical purpose such as screening the nest against the direct rays of the sun should not be removed permanently but can be drawn temporarily aside and tied to another branch until photography is complete, when they can be restored. It is also important that the nest and its surroundings appear as natural as possible in the viewfinder screen. That is to say, there must be no freshly-cut surfaces in evidence and severed twigs replaced in the bush must appear as natural as possible. Another aspect of gardening is the removal or screening of any feature which would, in the finished picture, constitute a distraction: a large leaf, for example, which just catches the light in such a way as to provide a blob of highlight should be removed or its stem bent so that the surface can be turned away.

Gardening should also be extended to any awkward objects between camera and nest which might provide a distracting out-of-focus foreground. There must be some foreground, of course, but it should, if possible, contribute to the composition of the picture and must not prompt the question from someone seeing the final picture, What's that in the foreground?

All these changes must be done as gradually as possible so as to minimize disturbance to the bird, and naturally nothing must be done which destroys the natural appearance of the nest and its surroundings.

The restoration of any vegetation removed or tied aside for photographic purposes is essential not only to provide shade, but also to hide the nest from enemies. The bird will have chosen the original site because of the cover it gave and it has the right to expect the cover to be made good every time the photographer ceases work either for the time being or altogether. To leave the nest exposed is to invite enemies.

DESERTING THE NEST

The danger of a subject deserting the nest because of the appearance near by of a hide is on the whole far less in the case of garden birds than it is when wild birds are the quarry. On the other hand every time a photographer intends to work at a nest, whether he uses a hide or not, there is the risk of the bird taking flight and abandoning the nest altogether. No bird would build in the garden at all if it had not already accepted man as a necessary part of its world. It will perhaps already be accustomed to seeing a man pass near the nest perhaps several times a day: it may even tolerate his doing some necessary gardening tasks in the vicinity without taking flight. In these circumstances the introduction of a hide may be a simple matter, but in all cases either the complete hide should be taken to the nest in easy stages, or it may be erected bit by bit in the final position. The photographer must use his judgment from previous observation of the bird's behaviour when he is near by.

When I have spotted an 'active' nest in the garden which I wish to photograph, I watch until the bird has returned to incubate and, when she appears to have settled, I deliberately walk past the nest, quietly and without turning my head: as though, in fact, I were far too intent on my own occupation to notice such a thing as a bird incubating. I do this several times a day, watching the bird's reaction out of the corner of my eye. If I am accepted as harmless I become bolder and may brush the lawn or do some other such job which involves not too noisy movement near the nest. If this is accepted, then I start building the hide within view of the bird but not too near the nest. If the bird takes fright I give up and try again. If she takes fright a second time I give up altogether.

Good manners should dictate one's behaviour on such occasions. It must be recognized that even if it is one's own garden, and one has full proprietorial rights over everything in it, the bird has built its nest at the invitation and encouragement of the garden's owner and to intrude on the guest's private affairs, particularly at such a vital stage in the bird's life cycle, is a breach of good manners and can only be done if the bird shows no resentment.

With some garden species many and sometimes all these precautions can be relaxed. But one should always start out by assuming the bird to be timid and shy and any relaxations must be done quietly and gently, as sudden movement even with the most tolerant of birds may drive them away for good.

CAN BIRDS COUNT?

Can birds count? The answer to this seems to vary. Some birds, particularly wild ones, if they see two humans approach a hide, will apparently not consider the coast clear until they also see two humans leave the hide. One way to overcome this is for the photographer to be accompanied to the hide by a helper, who subsequently leaves the photographer hidden and walks away holding a macintosh or similar coat at arm's-length. The bird, or some of them, see the two figures and believe the hide to be empty. I have never found it necessary to practise this kind of deception in the garden. But I have found that if I approach the hide alone and enter it, even when the bird is not incubating, it will be a very long time before the bird feels brave enough to approach the nest. I generally get someone to walk to the hide with me; I enter and my companion departs. This dodge seems to be quite enough. It never pays, however, to leave the hide by myself and so I arrange some kind of visual signal which tells my helper that I am ready to leave the hide.

SHUTTER NOISE AND FLASH

When photographing from a hide everything possible should be done to put the bird, whether nesting or not, at its ease. The shutters of some cameras, particularly of the reflex, are inclined to be noisy. Thus, if an exposure is made and a flash operated at the same time the bird may take fright. It is worth while firing the shutter a few times with no film in the camera to accustom the bird to the noise which at first will be strange to it since it does not occur in the normal world of sound to which the bird is accustomed. In this respect the coupled rangefinder camera is undoubtedly superior, in some makes the shutter operating with a faint click which is inaudible at a distance of a few feet.

The sudden bright light from a flash has a varying effect on birds. It frightens some away when feeding, but not for long and they never go far. Even the great spotted woodpecker merely dodges round behind the tree trunk to which the bait is fixed. Some birds, including the longtailed tit, merely look up to see where the lightning came from; and other birds ignore the flash altogether. In fact, they are less disturbed by it than they are by the click of the camera shutter.

3. *Blue tit.* Photographed through window glass on the perch described on p. 106, using the window hide (see p. 89), the technique discussed on p. 112 and the prefocusing card shown in Fig. 8. The bird is 2 ft. 3 in. from the camera and the main flash head. The cheese bait and auxiliary flash are to the left. *Leica* M2, *Visoflex* II, focusing bellows and optical section of 135-mm. *Elmar* lens at an effective aperture of about f/20. Ilford *Pan F* film.

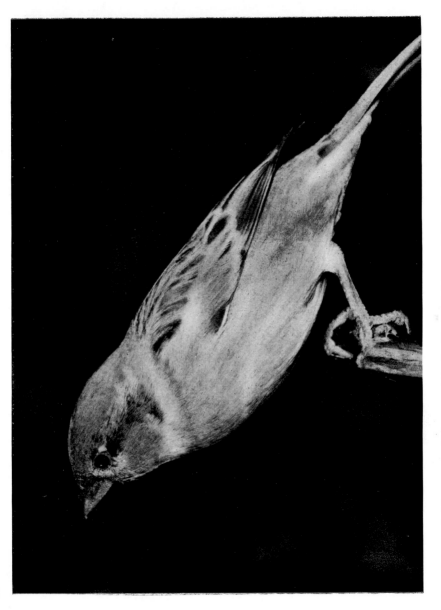

5. *Hen sparrow*. Data, except for the film (Kodak *Pantomic*-X) as for the blue tit (Plate 3).

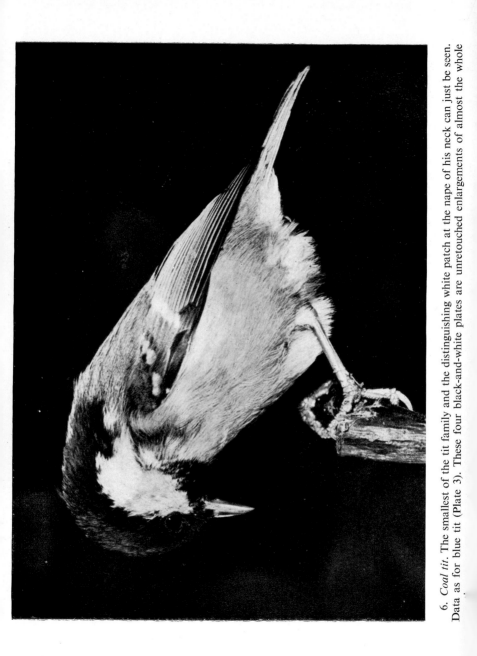

6. *Coal tit.* The smallest of the tit family and the distinguishing white patch at the nape of his neck can just be seen. Data as for blue tit (Plate 3). These four black-and-white plates are unretouched enlargements of almost the whole

Taking the Picture

If, too, the lid of a tin or some other bright object is fixed to the outside of the hide somewhere near the position to be occupied ultimately by the flash lamp, the bird will soon get used to it.

WAIT UNTIL THE BIRD SETTLES

The temptation to fire the shutter as soon as the bird has settled on the nest is very great, but it should be resisted. She may still be suspicious of the hide itself and you may be sure that she will be on the *qui vive* for any unusual sounds or sights until she has accepted the hide as a natural part of the surroundings. My observation of birds returning to brood eggs is that some will sit as soon as they reach the nest but very often after a few seconds or so they will rise, turn round and sit again as though they hadn't found the most comfortable position first time. The bird should be watched to see if she does this normally and, in any case she should be allowed several minutes' peace before a picture is taken. When she hears the shutter click she will almost certainly sit upright and look round; and if flash is used, she may either fly away or at least will appear restless and show other signs of agitation. When this happens no movement at all should be made until she settles again, when the shutter may be rewound. It is impossible to avoid all noises during the necessary operations of photographing from the hide, but they should be done as quietly as possible.

PHOTOGRAPHING AT FEEDING PLACES

When I first started garden bird photography, I used a small table to attract the birds, but soon found that it was unsuitable for several reasons. First, I could not secure a large enough image of any one bird because I had to include the entire table in the field of view; secondly, the piles of food, even though quite small, were unsightly; and third, the rim round the edge of the table obscured the birds' feet. Birds feeding on suspended coco-nuts present much the same kind of problem as the bird table. One cannot determine exactly where the bird will perch, or whether he will present his head, his tail or entire profile to the camera. In addition, while he may be in sharp focus on one side of the coco-nut, he will be out of focus on the other. At best, when he is actually feeding, it is more than likely that his head will be entirely out of sight. I then hit upon a plan which has worked very well and which I have used to take the majority of my close-ups. Instead of a table, I hollowed out to a depth of about 1 in. the end of a 3-in. diameter branch of alder. This was fixed into the ground at such a distance from a window that a bird of the size of a blackbird would fill the viewfinder when perched on either side of the branch so that he presented a sideways view. This bait served very well to photograph blackbirds, starlings, pairs of blue tits and long-tailed tits and others.

This bait has provided many opportunities for amusing studies of two birds feeding amicably together, as in the case of a pair of long-tailed tits or, much more often, of two birds threatening one another.

Close-ups of Small Birds

Growing more ambitious, I decided to try close-ups of small birds and this I managed in the following way. I moved the bait about a foot or so to one side of its former position and replaced it by a small perch not more than 2 in. long and set at right-angles to the window. The great majority of birds, seeing the cheese or other food in the bait, will not fly direct to it, but will alight first on the small perch from which the food is easily seen, although the bait is outside the camera's field of view. The perch was made large enough so that a bird had room enough for both feet but not so long that he could move sideways and thus get out of focus, which is critical at such short distances.

When it is proposed to have a session of bird photography using a perch as the 'studio'—in other words, to make a close-up of an individual bird—much time and material will be saved if we make sure that the bird fills the viewfinder frame and, if possible, that he is facing in the direction we want him to look. When using the small perch outside my window I can make almost certain on which side of the picture the head will appear by placing the food in its container on that side and about 1 ft. away. On that side, too, but about 4 ft. distant, is the auxiliary flash head. If the bird

Fig. 8. Outline on card for prefocusing on perch
for close-ups of passerines.

doesn't alight facing the food, he will certainly within a very short
time turn towards it. If no auxiliary flash is being used, then it
doesn't matter which way he looks so long as he presents a true
profile to the camera.

Prefocusing on a Perch

To make sure that I secure as large an image as possible of the
bird I proceed as follows. A rectangle is cut out of white cardboard, the longest side of which is to scale with the greatest dimension of the bird, i.e. tip of beak to end of tail. I generally leave
about an inch clearance all round as a margin of safety. The other
two sides of the rectangle are drawn in proportion to the shorter
side of the reversal or negative film. An example will show what I
mean. I use 35-mm. material exclusively, so that the overall size
of the picture is $1 \times 1\frac{1}{2}$ in. Suppose I'm trying to photograph a
robin which is, say, 6 in. long overall. On the basis of the 2 : 3
proportion of the $1 \times 1\frac{1}{2}$-in. frame, this would give me a rectangle
6×4 in. and, allowing for the 1-in. margin all round, I have a
rectangle measuring about 7×5 in. (Fig. 8). I accordingly draw
in ink a rectangle of this size on white cardboard with an outline
of, say, a house sparrow, not making the lines too thick because I

want as sharp a focus as possible. I then pierce a small hole near the bottom of the card so that I can push it on to the stick forming the perch. This is horizontal, about 2 in. long and at right-angles to the camera position. When the card is in the centre of the length of the stick, I focus on the rectangular outline, moving the camera to and fro until the outline just, and only just, disappears from sight in the viewfinder. I do this because, with my camera at any rate, I always get more on the film than I see on the ground-glass. I then make the final focusing adjustments until the outline of the bird is really sharp. The camera is then locked in position.

A rectangle of this size will do not only for the robin, but for the great tit, chaffinch, sparrow, dunnock, greenfinch, nuthatch and other small birds of similar size. In fact, most 'domestic' wild birds are of this size. Sometimes, of course, one of the tits, though alighting on the perch, will hang down from it instead of standing horizontally in the manner of the other birds. When this happens it just can't be helped and one must be patient in the hope that the tit will move to the required position, which he generally does before his final approach to the food.

Of course, birds of any size can be photographed in this way because the scale is determined by the distance of the perch or bait from the camera. But, naturally, if this distance is so set that it will accommodate, say, a blackbird, the smaller birds will appear as much smaller images. This may not matter: it depends entirely upon what the photographer is after.

The occasional visitor too large to frame in the viewfinder must either be scared away by operating the electronic flash independently of the camera shutter, or he must be endured.

As a rough and ready rule, garden birds fall into three classes so far as size is concerned. First, there is the 'robin' division just mentioned. Then there are the smaller birds, such as the wrens, blue tits, coal tits, marsh tits and willow warblers. The larger birds include blackbirds, thrushes, starlings and the great spotted woodpecker. Some birds are awkward, of course. There is the long-tailed tit which, though it has a tiny body has an overall length of about the same as the great tit. The really large birds, which are the most difficult to photograph, are the crow family, jays, magpies and the green woodpecker. As a general rule, however, most of the first three sizes mentioned above can be brought to some kind of bait to be photographed.

BAIT FOR THE NUTHATCH

When after the tits or nuthatch, I often use a different kind of bait. This is a smaller version of the drilled log described on p. 36, which is placed near the window in a vertical position. The rectangular outline is made large enough to contain the nuthatch and fixed to the side of the log to simulate the position the bird would be occupying when feeding on the nuts. The holes for the nuts are drilled in a single vertical line and the log so placed that the nuts inserted in the holes are broadside on to the camera. This log is kept fairly well stocked with nuts but, when the camera is set up, only the top holes are filled. An outline made big enough to accommodate the nuthatch will be too big for, say, the blue tit, but the chance of taking the nuthatch should not be missed because he is one of the loveliest birds to come to the garden and is nothing like so shy as the great spotted woodpecker.

PHOTOGRAPHING WOODPECKERS

The great spotted woodpecker is too shy to come so close to the window and must be photographed on a tree. In his case the cardboard rectangle (Fig. 9) is set in the position he occupies when feeding but with the longer dimension vertical. For his pictures I use the simple type of hide already described, i.e. the one that conceals the camera and flash equipment, but not the flash head itself. My earlier great spotted woodpecker pictures were taken with an *Exakta* VXIIa mounted on *Novoflex* bellows, using the British *Trinol* 105-mm. f/3·5 lens. This lens has no focusing mount, the optical section only being fitted to the front of the bellows. To focus the great spotted woodpecker rectangle, the back of the camera, i.e. the film plane, has to be 42 in. from the cardboard outline, the bellows being extended to the point engraved '1·2' on the rack. With such a set-up a rectangle 12 × 8 in. exactly fills the ground-glass screen. With daylight *Kodachrome* I

FIG. 9. Outline on card for taking close-ups of the great spotted woodpecker at the bait.

and an outdoor flash factor of 30 and taking into account the bellows extension which of course reduces the effective lens aperture below that engraved on the lens mount, the lens is closed to slightly over f/6·3 to give an effective aperture of about f/7·5 (see Table 12). I should mention that the flash head is at the same distance from the target as the camera, but at an angle of 30 degrees with the camera-object axis, while the auxiliary flash head is carried on a bamboo stake at right-angles to the camera-object axis and about 4 ft. from the bait.

For covering an area on the viewfinder large enough to take in the great spotted woodpecker and birds of similar size—that is to say a rectangle of about 12 × 8 in.—the camera is not in the strict sense being used for close-up work. With the 105-mm. lens mentioned, the bellows must be almost fully retracted and there might be the danger of light being reflected from the edges of the closely packed folds. If there is any danger from this, one can sometimes use a lens of longer focal length in conjunction with extension tubes or rings to permit a closer approach to the bird.

Taking the Picture

One must naturally take into account the effect of the tubes on the effective aperture of the lens, but makers of these devices issue tables which give the necessary information. An example may show what I mean by this. I have a 135-mm. f/4 *Sonnar* of rather ancient vintage which has been adapted to fit the *Exakta* bayonet. If the pair of adaptor rings from the standard set of *Exakta* extension tubes is fitted to this lens, the 12 × 8-in. area to cover the woodpecker is included at a distance of 4 ft. 6 in. from the front of the lens, which means only 1 ft. farther away than is possible with the 105-mm. lens and bellows, but that extra small distance may mean greater peace of mind for the bird.

I might mention here a point in connection with photographing the great spotted woodpecker with flash. If he scuttles around the back of the tree when the shutter is fired, I don't disturb him and hope he will return to feed. On other occasions he flies off to a nearby tree. If I immediately emerge from hiding to wind the shutter he flies right away and may not return all day. But if I content myself with the one exposure for the time being and make no attempt to approach the camera he apparently decides that what he heard and saw were no great cause for alarm and he soon returns. I then allow him to complete his meal in peace because it has occurred to me that he may have been learning to identify the click of the shutter and the flash as a preliminary warning of my approach.

GROUND BAIT

If some kind of ground bait is being used to attract birds, there is always the problem of scaring away the unwanted ones such as sparrows and starlings. If one is in the hide oneself and not merely operating the camera by means of a long shutter release, the desired effect can often be obtained by firing the flash by hand which, on the *Mecablitz*, can be done by pressing a small button on the flash-head shaft. One must not do this too often, however, because of running down the cells. But if the flash set is plugged into the domestic electricity mains, one can operate the flash as often as one wishes without detriment. Incidentally, when using my hide within 30 yards of the house I always keep it plugged into

111

the mains by a lead of the necessary length. If one has electric light in a toolshed or garage well away from the house, it might be possible always to operate an electronic flash from the mains and at the same time keep the cells fully charged.

Photographing through a closed window is perfectly feasible; in fact, this is how the greater part of my bird photography is done. But there are one or two points which must be borne in mind. First, the glass must be spotlessly clean and there must be no flaws in it which come within the view of the lens. Secondly, the camera and flash, where this is used, must be so positioned that no reflection of the camera is seen in the finished photograph or transparency. Many of my first shots, though otherwise successful, were ruined because the image of the lens sunshade was visible. I overcame this by moving the camera nearer, almost touching, the glass, and shifted the perch farther back so as to keep it at the proper distance from the camera. As a general rule, the window glass itself provides enough cover not to frighten the bird, but to make sure I generally drape a piece of soft black cloth over the camera to hide the bright metal parts, or I use the hide mentioned on p. 89. The head of the flash unit, of course, must be left clear so that the beam of light is in no way impeded.

To obtain as 'round' a picture of the bird as possible, it is always a good plan to use an auxiliary flash head at nearly right-angles to the main flash. In my case, this auxiliary has to be placed outdoors, so that its use in bad weather is impossible, because one of the most harmful things to flash equipment, apart from mishandling, is moisture in any form. In spite of what some authorities say to the contrary, I never take the auxiliary flash head into consideration when working out the lens aperture and flash distance. I base my calculations entirely on the distance of the main flash from the perch, measuring it with a steel tape of the kind that remains straight as you pull it out. The measurement is always made from the centre of the perch to the back of the flash reflector.

Sometimes the flash startles the bird, but not enough to drive it away. The problem then is to wind on the film and set the shutter,

Taking the Picture

which means approaching the window and probably scaring away the sitter. A way to overcome this is to have a piece of black cloth drawing-pinned across the window with holes cut for the camera lens and the flash lamp. This gives cover while approaching the window.

At first I had difficulty with a suitable camera support. As the front of the lens must be near the window which has a sill about 8 in. wide, the ordinary tripod was out of the question because it held the camera too far away from the glass. Next I tried my Leitz table tripod with ball-and-socket head. This was quite rigid enough to hold both camera and bellows but, as the window-sill was highly polished I was afraid of some clumsy movement of mine bringing the whole thing down on the floor. I got over this difficulty by buying from a dealer one of those heavy metal brass plates with a threaded projection in the centre which they use for displaying cameras in their windows. The threaded projection carries the Leitz ball-and-socket head which in turn supports the camera and bellows, giving me a heavy and perfectly rigid assembly, no part of which sticks out into the room. It is absolutely essential to have some such arrangement, i.e. one not easily upset, where there may be a trailing cable to the flash equipment and a long shutter release. Tripping up over either of these could bring disaster to any apparatus not solidly supported.

BACKGROUNDS

When making a close-up of a bird on a perch, the question of a background may be important. Unless the weather is bright, the use of flash will almost invariably mean that the bird will appear against an almost completely black background. This will naturally enhance the bird's colours, but it is sometimes objected to because the picture may give the impression of an exposure made at night. This is only the case if the perch is specially designed for bird close-ups and stands isolated from leaves, twigs or other vegetation. Some photographers take the trouble to rig up a special sheet of some colour near enough to the perch to be lit by the flash and perhaps to provide a contrasting hue to the main overall colour of the subject. If this idea is used, the sheet should

H   113

be preferably of green or blue, i.e. one of the so-called 'cold' colours. The photographer must naturally take the risk of birds being scared away by any such artificial background, because it is unlikely to be left in position long enough for the birds to become accustomed to it.

I have never used a background of this type and if a natural one in the form of some kind of vegetation does not happen to be in the right place, I don't bother. One of the perches I use for studio has a rose bush 2 ft. behind it, which serves very well to break up the blackness because it receives some illumination from the flash head alongside the camera.

The only exception I have made has been when the hollowed-out top of an alder branch provides a studio for close-ups. As explained in a previous chapter the hollow provides a kind of cup about 2 in. diameter with a narrow rim upon which the bird stands while feeding on the cheese. This bait is used to give a profile of the bird large enough to fill the 35-mm. frame. Obviously, the bird can in the ordinary way perch anywhere round the rim of this cup in such a way that the camera might get a head-on or, say, a three-quarters view, neither of which is suitable, either pictorially or technically, because of the depth-of-field problem. To ensure that the bird stands sideways to the camera, I have sometimes tacked a large twig of cypress to the back of the 'cup' in such a way that if the bird wants the cheese he must present his profile to the lens. He could, of course, perch with his tail towards the camera, but he won't do this because the window through which the camera is peering at him might hide a potential enemy. An easier way of getting a large profile image of a bird, however, is to use the short perch, already described, upon which most birds alight on their way to the cheese bait.

SETTING UP THE EQUIPMENT

Even after several years' experience in close-up photography of birds I find it necessary to have a permanent list of the steps to be taken in setting up equipment, whether for indoors or out. These are the stages:

Taking the Picture

1. Set camera on tripod or other support and roughly focus on the bait. Mark the position carefully.
2. Erect the hide at such a distance from the bait and in such a position that the camera has a clear view.
3. Fix the flash head in position on a second tripod or other support.
4. Connect the flash socket to the domestic mains, if this method of working is being used, as it nearly always is when photographing from indoors or from a position near the house.
5. Fix the auxiliary flash head into the set and point at the bait.
6. Connect the main flash head to the X-socket on the camera.
7. Connect the long shutter release to the camera.
8. Measure the distance exactly from the bait to the back of the main flash reflector.
9. Focus exactly on the bait and lock the bellows in position.
10. Set the lens to the correct aperture, taking into account the guide number being used and the amount by which the effective lens aperture is reduced by the bellows extension. This effective aperture is obtained from the calibrations on the bellows guide rail. An example from my own experience will illustrate what I mean. When photographing from a window with the bellows set to take in the whole length of, say, a great tit or bird of similar size, the bellows calibration reads 1·2. Using a guide number of 25 to 30 for daylight *Kodachrome*, the figure I find most suitable for outdoor work would, without the bellows, mean setting the aperture at f/8. The bellows extension, however, at 1·2 reduces f/8 to f/9·6, obtained by the simple process of multiplying 8 × 1·2. The marked aperture, then, is closed down to about f/7 or just under f/8.
11. Switch on the electricity supply to the flash. When the indicator tubes are both glowing, test-fire the flash by pressing the button on the flash head.

All is now set for photography. The procedure, no doubt, sounds rather elaborate but only, I think, because I have included explanatory notes under each head. It is, however, well worth while making a similar list of the jobs to be done in correct order. In my case it saves a lot of time, because if I forget anything I have to climb upstairs to fetch it. It is the small objects that need listing,

115

particularly the tape or rule for measuring distances. I always had to make a separate journey for this until I worked from a list.

It will be seen that when bellows are used, the extension must be taken into account when working out the effective lens aperture. However, it is easy to make a table of these effective apertures at various bellows extensions, and to illustrate the point I have included my own table (Table 12). My equipment for photographing birds at close range, as I have said elsewhere, includes an *Exakta, Novoflex* bellows and the 105-mm. f/3·5 *Trinol* lens without focusing mount. The optical section of the *Trinol* which is the lens without focusing mount, has a *Leica* thread and is attached to the *Exakta* bayonet on the front of the bellows via a *Novoflex EXLEI* adaptor. I have made tables for each of the lenses used with the bellows and they do save time in close-up work, which has quite enough problems already until one becomes used to it. I have also made a table for the 135-mm. *Elmar* referred to on p. 14.

When photographing from the complete hide, of course, the hide should already be in position for a day or so before any photography is attempted. When step (1) above is taken, therefore, the camera is brought away again after the right position of the hide has been fixed, and no attempt should be made to set up any equipment at all until it is evident that the quarry has decided that the new feature of the landscape can be ignored.

All this, of course, does take time, and I usually estimate 25 to 20 minutes to have everything in readiness for the birds. The ideal would be a study or playroom on the ground floor of the house, from which photography could be done and in which all the equipment could be stored. Some of it, in fact, could be left *in situ* covered with large polythene bags or a light cloth. If a polythene bag is used, on no account should it be completely enclosed or moisture present will not be able to get out and will condense on the equipment. An inverted bag with the bottom left open is quite enough to keep the worst of the dust off.

If one is photographing birds just outside the window it is unnecessary to watch all the time. I manage to occupy myself with other tasks, provided they are sedentary, because I am within 8 ft. or so of the bait and not hidden in the strict sense, but I am

Taking the Picture

able to type, write or read a book, giving an occasional glance to see if there is something to 'shoot'. If the bait takes the form of peanuts the birds betray their presence by the noise made when pecking at the shells.

WINNING THE BIRDS' CONFIDENCE

It is worth while trying to win the confidence of the birds it is desired to photograph, or at any rate to remove some of the natural fear they have of man. Because of this no attempt should be made to take pictures when a new perch or other site is first put into position. The birds should be allowed to become accustomed to the 'studio' and to take their food in peace because if on their first visit to the perch they are greeted with electronic flashes and clicking shutters they may be scared off for good. However great the temptation to take pictures it should at first be resisted.

Photographing the nuthatch is an example. Careful placing of the bait is necessary to induce him to take up a suitable position for a profile view. But do not be too impatient to operate the shutter. If he is at work on a peanut let him get down to the job properly and if possible allow him to make enough progress with cracking the shell to see the nut within. Then if he is scared off by the shutter noise and flash he will be more eager to return for his prize. The nuthatch is a restless bird, his movements being very rapid and sudden. But it will be noticed that every now and then he pauses for breath or contemplation and this is the time to 'shoot' him. But always be patient and wait for the best views which he will sooner or later assume if the bait is correctly placed.

It is a good plan, however, to have the camera in place as if to photograph and, from a hide, to study the position taken up by the birds to see whether on the whole they present the best view of themselves and whether they fill the viewfinder frame. It will often be found that a slight alteration to the position of either the perch or the camera or both will make photography easier or yield a better picture. The perch, at least, should be firmly fixed when the best place is found; and it is easy enough to devise some way of marking the best place for the camera. Setting up the equipment takes some time in any case, especially if flash is to be used, so that if the relative positions of camera and perch are fixed and known it will be of considerable help.

I do much of my close-up work from the window-sill, the perch being outside the window, of course, and fixed firmly in position. I have cut out a piece of brown paper the exact size of the window-sill and the outline of the camera support is traced on it in ink. I can thus put the camera straight into position and all that is needed is the final critical focusing. In the case of outdoor hides, when they get in the way of grass-cutting or other routine jobs, short stakes are inserted in the holes made by the front pair of uprights, so that the hide can at once be restored to its proper position.

CHAPTER 7

Some Afterthoughts

If this has seemed rather a solemn book on such a simple hobby as photographing birds in one's own garden, it is because for best results the hobby has to be taken seriously. That is to say, no one can hope to produce a first-class portrait of a bird, or indeed of any other object, unless he takes the utmost care, first, in stalking his quarry or bringing it to the bait; and secondly, in setting up his equipment and focusing his camera. Whatever type of apparatus is used, close-up pictures of any subject mean a small depth of field, and that in turn requires extremely careful focusing. If flash is used, distances must be accurate and, if a bellows or tube extension is involved, effective lens apertures must be calculated. The many other factors incidental to making a satisfactory picture must also have their due attention. Any keen photographer knows this and, though he takes this part of the art seriously, the labour involved is far from being onerous and is as full of interest as any other kind of picture-making.

The very fact that I wished to photograph my garden birds led me inevitably to study them because, as I have already said, one must know something of the habits and characteristics of the different species to make photography of them possible. Some birds always feed on the ground, so it is waste of time trying to attract them to a perch. Others, such as the members of the tit family, can be photographed hanging upside down or clinging to the trunk of a tree. They rarely feed on the ground. The great spotted woodpecker prefers to feed in the same way, though hanging upside down on the bottom of a food basket is not natural for him and he seems uncomfortable in that position. He likes his bait tucked into a crevice in the bark of a tree and I have noticed that he likes to feed vertically, i.e. straight up and down, which is very convenient for photography, as my frontispiece shows. The nuthatch is equally at home upside down as right side up or sideways, and photographing him really close up is not always easy, but it can be done as will be seen from one of my pictures. These are a few examples of what one discovers when studying birds for photography. And this is only a part of the fun which can be had from the hobby. In other words, studying birds as one would study any other sitter for a portrait sharpens the observation and the more one observes the more will one enjoy the subjects one is watching.

Watching from a hide of the kind shown in Fig. 6, or through a window, gives endless opportunities for seeing these lovely wild creatures at close range, especially if one has a pair of binoculars, even if for the moment one is not photographing them. The beautiful colours of their plumage when seen close to is entrancing and, instead of having an overall impression of a single, perhaps rather drab, colour, as one so often does when seeing a small bird a few yards away, when within a couple of feet of the same bird one discovers many sub-hues in the plumage. The greenfinch and the chaffinch are examples of birds which improve immensely on close inspection. Of course, this is why close-up photography of even the most ordinary garden birds is so absorbing: their images when projected on a screen will astonish many people who had not realized how complex is the pattern and colour of even the commonest species.

The bird photographer, sitting behind a window with a camera shutter release in his hand (the easiest and most comfortable way of photographing birds), waiting for a subject to come to a bait, will observe a number of other things about the birds in his garden. Why, for instance, do thrushes seem to arrive on the lawn or other feeding place after all the others have been at it for some time, thus losing the tastiest morsels? Why do young chaffinches, about to be fed by a parent, wag their heads rapidly from side to side, thus slowing up the feeding process? Why, when the lawn is liberally sprinkled with food, and all the other birds are stuffing themselves, do cock blackbirds indulge in a game of tag? These are just some of the questions I would like answered, but ornith-

Some Afterthoughts

ologists as a rule seem to be strictly objective when contemplating birds, and my questions are no doubt too frivolous to be taken seriously. But I would far rather know why these things happen than be told the reasons for labelling the wren *Troglodytes troglodytes* and the robin *Erithacus rubecula*.

These quirks of behaviour are not a characteristic of the starling (*Sturnus vulgaris*). When the starling sees food he makes a bee-line for it and gobbles until it has all gone. If the reader is as plagued with starlings as I am, he will soon discover that nothing defeats them except wire netting of 1½-in. mesh or smaller. My starlings have learnt to hang upside down on the wire basket to take the food put out for the tits and to cling to a tree trunk to steal the bait for the great spotted woodpecker. They are the most frequent bathers in the garden and in hard weather they perch in the surrounding trees waiting for me to break the ice on the pond. Though they are quarrelsome among themselves and make a great noise about it, they do not seem to bully the smaller birds. Finally, the starling, whatever his objectionable habits, is one of the most graceful birds in flight, as anyone will know who has seen them returning to London and other cities as soon as dusk falls. But this bird, like the sparrow, should never be encouraged. Their nests should be destroyed, except, of course, if they contain young.

I've said very little about predators in the body of the book, but the photographer who attracts birds to his garden mainly, it must be admitted, for his own enjoyment, is under an obligation to protect them so far as he can. Birds are most vulnerable when in the nest, so nest boxes and other artificial sites must be made as inaccessible as possible to cats, squirrels and other creatures who prey upon small birds. I have already said before that enclosed nest boxes of the type made for tits must be of adequate depth so that not even the longest arm of the largest cat can reach the nestlings through the entrance hole. Open boxes and other artificial sites are more difficult to protect, and so are the nests built on the ground. Open boxes should if possible be made difficult of access, except by the birds themselves. Almost nothing can be done about ground nests except to avoid drawing attention to them by too frequent visits, and they should not be surrounded by chicken wire because cats will investigate some such strange phenomenon.

Apart from the occasional kestrel snatching a bird from a flock feeding on the lawn, the worst predators I have to try and defend my birds against are cats and grey squirrels. Jays and magpies do visit the garden, but I'm not aware of any nest being robbed by them. So far as cats are concerned, I am generally warned by the blackbirds if one is about and I keep a pile of small stones handy to scare him off: occasionally I have been too late. I have also stoned squirrels and driven them away but they are more persistent than cats. I believe grey squirrels should be shot, but if they are they must be killed and not allowed to escape wounded. In any case, the local police should always be consulted before any kind of a firearm is used, even an air gun. If the squirrel is hit, no one else can be injured but, if it is missed and one lives in a crowded neighbourhood as I do, all sorts of trouble might ensue.

Every photographer of garden birds will have his frustrations and amusing experiences, and they are all a part of the game. When I started photographing birds from a window, I tried it with the window open so as not to have any glass between the lens and the bird. My first sitter, the easiest of all, was a robin. I arranged the perch, focused on it and then placed small pieces of cheese in such a position that the shortest, quickest and safest route to the bait from any part of the garden was via the perch. But the robin didn't think so. He flew straight through the open window to the camera, perched on it for a few seconds, and thence to the cheese, while I sat in the room, shutter release at the ready. He refused to use the perch at all until I closed the window and photographed him through the glass.

When I first tried to take the nuthatch, I set up the camera and flash outdoors without any kind of hide as he seemed so tame. Every time he got himself in the target area and I fired shutter and flash, he flew from the bait to one of the metal tripod legs. As this was too smooth for him to grip, he slid slowly to the ground. As soon as he reached the grass he flew back to the bait. This happened on several successive visits.

One of the most colourful of 'my' birds is the young great spotted woodpecker at the stage when he appears to be wearing a bright red beret. He is less timid than his parents and I have often photographed him on the trunk of a crab tree with the hide for camera and flash shown in Fig. 7. One of these young birds, like the nuthatch, behaved in a most amusing way when I fired the shutter and flash at him. Instead of flying away or retreating sideways round the trunk of the tree as his parents do, he flew the few feet to the hide to investigate the source of the disturbance. He alighted on the top bar of the hide, hopped sideways along it, and from there on to one of the tripod legs. Shortly after he was lost to sight, but I could hear loud tappings coming apparently from under that part of the fabric covering the top of the camera. I quickly went over in my mind what damage he could do, but decided that so long as he didn't peck a hole in my precious bellows, all should be well. So I let him be. Apparently satisfied that there was nothing so tasty under the hide as there was on the tree, he returned to the bait. It was a full ten minutes before he left and I could go out to look for damage, but there was no mark of any sort.

Young great and blue tits are also very inquisitive. The auxiliary head of my flash set, which of course cannot be hidden, fascinates them, and they are for ever pecking at the bright bowl of the reflector and at the tube itself. One could go on recounting such episodes indefinitely and I often wish I had made notes at the time of bird behaviour while watching and waiting for a suitable sitter to pose in the right place. But anyone who has done this kind of photography will have his own anecdotes to relate, because to photograph birds means necessarily to study them and to study them is to discover for oneself many apparent oddities of behaviour—their feeding and bathing habits, their selfless devotion to their young and their persistence when they have spotted what seems to them the ideal nesting site, but which to us appears foolhardy and inviting depredation and destruction. Blackbirds seem to be particularly stupid in this respect.

I have tried to emphasize here and there that the most unforgivable thing one can do is to expose garden birds, or any others for that matter, to predators. I have seen some grisly examples of photographs of nesting birds where the gardening has been so drastic that the nestlings have been deprived entirely of protection either from the sun or from predators. One should, I suppose, not be too sentimental, but some books are illustrated by photographs, excellent technically, but which show clearly that the photographer has sacrificed his subjects to his camera. He has his picture and the birds can go hang. He has relied on the devotion of parent birds to give him the kind of picture he wants. This callousness cannot be too strongly condemned.

I hope any readers who think of following my example will derive as much fun from photographing the birds in their gardens as I have. There is, in fact, no need for the would-be bird photographer to go trekking off into the wilds in search of his subjects: they are right in his own garden or backyard. And, though such birds may not at first seem very exciting as subjects for the camera, believe me this is by no means the case. Inducing them to pose for the camera opens up an entirely new field of interest and instruction and is a hobby which can be pursued by anyone with the cheapest of cameras all the year round, both indoors and out. Of all the forms of hunting wild animals, stalking them or 'trapping' them on a perch with a 35-mm. camera is, in my opinion, incomparably the best.

Index

Index

Index